# DIABETIC

## DIET COOKBOOK

## for Beginners

MASTER PREDIABETES, DIABETES, AND TYPE 2 DIABETES WITH 100 DELICIOUS LOW-CARB AND LOW-SUGAR RECIPES, ALL IN FULL COLOR. INCLUDES A 28-DAY EATING PLAN.

Gertraud Kron

This document is intended to provide accurate and reliable information regarding the subject matter discussed.

# Sommario

# Chapter 1: Introduction

Welcome to *Diabetic Diet for Beginners*. If you or a loved one has been diagnosed with diabetes, navigating the new reality of dietary management can seem daunting. This book is designed to simplify that journey, providing you with a solid foundation of knowledge to manage diabetes effectively through diet.

## Understanding Diabetes

Diabetes is a chronic condition characterized by high levels of sugar (glucose) in the blood. It occurs when the body either does not produce enough insulin (Type 1 Diabetes) or cannot effectively use the insulin it does produce (Type 2 Diabetes). Managing blood sugar levels is crucial, as uncontrolled levels can lead to severe health complications over time.

## The Role of Diet in Diabetes Management

Diet plays a pivotal role in managing diabetes. The right foods can help stabilize blood sugar levels, while the wrong ones can cause dangerous spikes or drops. Understanding which foods to eat, which to avoid, and how to balance meals is essential. This book aims to demystify these concepts and provide you with practical, easy-to-follow guidelines.

## What You Will Learn

This book covers various critical aspects of a diabetic diet, including:

- **The Basics of Nutrition:** Learn about carbohydrates, proteins, and fats, and their effects on blood sugar levels.
- **Foods to Embrace and Avoid:** We'll explore which foods can help stabilize your glucose and which might cause harmful fluctuations.
- **Meal Planning Strategies:** Gain insights into planning your meals effectively to maintain steady blood sugar throughout the day.
- **Portion Control:** Discover how to measure and control portion sizes that align with your health needs without feeling deprived.
- **Reading Food Labels:** Learn how to read and understand food labels, helping you make informed choices when shopping.

## Empowering Yourself Through Education

This chapter sets the stage for a deeper understanding of how diabetes interacts with diet. By educating yourself, you become empowered to make choices that enhance your well-being. Managing diabetes doesn't mean giving up all the foods you love; it's about learning to enjoy them in a way that also respects your body's needs.

## The Journey Ahead

As you progress through *Diabetic Diet for Beginners*, you'll find comprehensive details on how to integrate these practices into your everyday life. Each chapter builds on the last, forming a complete picture of how to live a full, healthy life with diabetes.

This introduction is just the beginning. With each page, you'll gain more tools and knowledge, easing the management of diabetes through informed, healthy eating choices. Whether you're newly diagnosed or looking to refine your dietary approach, this book is a step toward healthier living.

Let's embark on this journey together, with the goal of not just living with diabetes, but thriving with it.

# Chapter 2: Causes and Types of Diabetes

Understanding the causes and different types of diabetes is crucial for anyone beginning to navigate their dietary management. This knowledge not only helps in understanding why certain dietary choices are necessary but also tailors management strategies to fit specific diabetic conditions. This chapter explores the underlying causes of diabetes and delineates the characteristics of its various types.

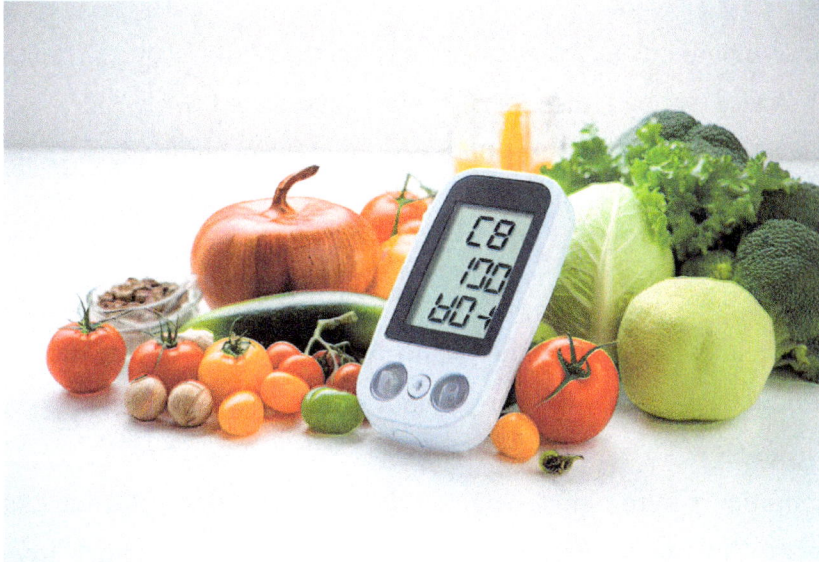

## Understanding the Causes of Diabetes

Diabetes develops due to issues with insulin production or function. Insulin is a hormone produced by the pancreas that helps glucose enter cells to be used for energy. When this process fails, glucose accumulates in the bloodstream, leading to high blood sugar levels.

**Genetic Factors**

Genetics play a significant role in the development of diabetes, particularly Type 1. If a family member has diabetes, the risk of developing it increases. However, genetic predisposition doesn't guarantee diabetes; lifestyle factors are also significant contributors.

**Environmental Triggers**

In Type 1 diabetes, an autoimmune response, possibly triggered by a viral infection, can cause the body to attack its insulin-producing cells. For Type 2, lifestyle factors such as poor diet, lack of exercise, and being overweight are major contributors. These factors lead to insulin resistance, where the body's cells do not respond effectively to insulin.

**Hormonal Changes**

Certain conditions like gestational diabetes arise during pregnancy due to hormonal changes that cause insulin resistance. Though often temporary, gestational diabetes exposes both mother and child to a higher risk of developing Type 2 diabetes later in life.

# Types of Diabetes

### Type 1 Diabetes

Type 1 diabetes is an autoimmune condition where the body's immune system attacks the pancreatic cells that produce insulin. It often develops early in life and requires daily insulin administration. Dietary management focuses on balancing insulin with food intake to maintain blood glucose levels.

### Type 2 Diabetes

The most common form of diabetes, Type 2, occurs when the body becomes resistant to insulin or when the pancreas cannot produce enough insulin. It's often associated with older age, obesity, and physical inactivity. Dietary strategies involve controlling portions, choosing foods with a low glycemic index, and managing calorie intake.

### Gestational Diabetes

This type affects some women during pregnancy and usually disappears after childbirth. However, it requires careful management to protect the health of both mother and baby. Diet plays a critical role in managing this type of diabetes, with a focus on balanced meals and monitoring blood sugar levels.

### Prediabetes

Prediabetes is a condition where blood sugar levels are higher than normal but not high enough to be classified as diabetes. This stage offers a critical opportunity for dietary intervention to prevent the progression to Type 2 diabetes.

# Why Diet Matters

Each type of diabetes has unique management needs, but all benefit significantly from dietary adjustments. Proper diet helps:

- Stabilize blood sugar levels.
- Reduce the risk of diabetes-related complications.
- Enhance overall health and energy levels.

### Conclusion

This chapter aims to build a foundational understanding of the physiological and environmental causes of diabetes and the differences between its types. With this knowledge, individuals can better understand their condition and the critical role diet plays in managing it. In the next chapters, we will delve into specific dietary strategies and how they can be applied to daily living to manage and possibly prevent diabetes effectively. This journey through understanding is the first step toward empowered, health-conscious living with diabetes.

# Chapter 3: Benefits of a Diabetic Diet

Adopting a diabetic diet isn't just about managing blood sugar—it's about transforming your overall health and well-being. This chapter highlights the multiple benefits of following a diabetic diet, which extend beyond glycemic control to improve various aspects of physical and mental health. Understanding these benefits can motivate adherence to dietary guidelines and promote a more holistic approach to diabetes management.

## Improved Blood Sugar Management

The primary aim of a diabetic diet is to maintain stable blood sugar levels. By focusing on low glycemic index foods, balanced meal timing, and appropriate portion sizes, this diet helps minimize the peaks and valleys in blood glucose that can lead to complications over time.

**Key aspects include:**

- **Consistent Carbohydrate Intake:** Helps in reducing glucose spikes.
- **Fiber-Rich Foods:** Slows the absorption of sugar, stabilizing blood sugar levels.
- **Healthy Fats and Lean Proteins:** Aid in prolonging satiety and preventing overeating.

## Enhanced Heart Health

People with diabetes are at a higher risk for heart disease. A diabetic diet rich in fruits, vegetables, lean proteins, and whole grains can reduce this risk by improving blood pressure, lowering cholesterol levels, and reducing arterial inflammation.

**Benefits for heart health include:**

- **Reduced Saturated and Trans Fat Intake:** Lowers bad cholesterol levels (LDL) and raises good cholesterol levels (HDL).
- **Increased Intake of Omega-3 Fatty Acids:** Found in fish and flaxseeds, omega-3s help reduce the risk of arrhythmias and atherosclerosis.

## Weight Management

Obesity is a significant risk factor for Type 2 diabetes. A diabetic diet, when followed in the context of controlled portions and regular physical activity, can lead to weight loss and better weight management, which is critical in reducing insulin resistance.

**Strategies for weight management:**

- **Caloric Control:** Tailoring daily caloric intake to individual needs helps in gradual and sustainable weight loss.
- **Balanced Meals:** Ensuring each meal has a good mix of nutrients to control hunger and cravings.

# Prevention of Diabetes-Related Complications

Proper diet can significantly reduce the risk of severe diabetes complications such as kidney disease, eye issues, and nerve damage. By controlling blood sugar, blood pressure, and cholesterol, a diabetic diet acts as a preventive tool against these conditions.

# Boost in Energy and Overall Well-being

Fluctuations in blood glucose levels can lead to energy spikes and crashes, affecting overall vitality. A balanced diabetic diet promotes a steady energy supply throughout the day, enhancing physical and mental energy levels.

**Improvements include:**

- **Enhanced Mood:** Stable blood sugar levels can improve mood and reduce the risk of depression associated with diabetes.
- **Better Cognitive Function:** A diet rich in nutrients supports cognitive functions and reduces the risk of diabetes-related cognitive decline.

**Conclusion**

The benefits of a diabetic diet extend far beyond simple blood sugar management. By adopting this dietary approach, individuals with diabetes can improve their heart health, manage their weight, prevent serious complications, and enjoy a higher quality of life. The subsequent chapters will provide detailed guidance on implementing these dietary changes, complete with practical tips and recipes to help integrate these principles into everyday life. This comprehensive approach ensures that each reader is equipped not just to manage diabetes but to thrive despite it.

# Chapter 4: Shopping List – Foods to Eat and Foods to Avoid

Creating a tailored shopping list is an essential step for anyone managing diabetes through diet. This chapter provides a detailed guide on which foods to embrace and which to limit or avoid. By knowing exactly what to put in your cart, you can ensure your meals are nutritious, delicious, and supportive of your diabetic health goals.

## Foods to Eat

A diabetes-friendly shopping list focuses on whole, nutrient-dense foods that help maintain stable blood sugar levels. Here's what to prioritize:

### 1. Whole Grains

- **Examples:** Quinoa, brown rice, whole wheat, barley, and oats.
- **Benefits:** These grains have a low glycemic index and provide sustained energy by releasing glucose slowly into the bloodstream.

### 2. Fruits and Vegetables

- **Examples:** Leafy greens (spinach, kale), berries, apples, and non-starchy vegetables like bell peppers and broccoli.
- **Benefits:** High in fiber, vitamins, and minerals, with minimal impact on blood sugar levels when portioned correctly.

### 3. Lean Proteins

- **Examples:** Chicken breast, turkey, fish (especially fatty fish like salmon and mackerel), tofu, and legumes.
- **Benefits:** Essential for muscle repair and maintenance without spiking blood sugar.

### 4. Dairy or Dairy Alternatives

- **Examples:** Low-fat milk, Greek yogurt, and unsweetened almond or soy milk.
- **Benefits:** Good sources of calcium and protein, choose low-fat options to reduce saturated fat intake.

### 5. Healthy Fats

- **Examples:** Avocados, nuts, seeds, and olive oil.
- **Benefits:** Help absorb vitamins and stabilize blood sugar levels; focus on monounsaturated and polyunsaturated fats.

### 6. Legumes

- **Examples:** Lentils, chickpeas, and black beans.
- **Benefits:** Rich in fiber and protein, help regulate blood sugar and are heart-healthy.

# Foods to Avoid

To manage diabetes effectively, it's just as important to know which foods to limit or avoid as it is to know which to consume:

**1. Refined Grains**

- **Examples:** White bread, white rice, and any products made with refined flour.
- **Benefits of Avoiding:** These foods can cause blood sugar levels to spike due to their high glycemic index.

**2. Sugary Snacks and Beverages**

- **Examples:** Soda, candy, ice cream, and pastries.
- **Benefits of Avoiding:** High in sugar and fast-digesting carbs, these can lead to rapid increases in blood glucose.

**3. High-Fat Animal Products**

- **Examples:** Fatty cuts of meat, bacon, and regular cheese.
- **Benefits of Avoiding:** Reduces intake of saturated fats, helping manage cholesterol levels, which is important for heart health.

**4. Deep-Fried and Processed Foods**

- **Examples:** French fries, chips, and processed meats like sausages.
- **Benefits of Avoiding:** These foods are not only high in unhealthy fats but often contain a lot of salt and additives, contributing to cardiovascular risk.

**5. Alcoholic Beverages**

- **Recommendation:** If consumed, should be in moderation.
- **Benefits of Avoiding:** Alcohol can cause unpredictable fluctuations in blood sugar levels and interfere with diabetes medications.

**Conclusion**

This chapter arms you with a clear, concise shopping list that aligns with the dietary needs of managing diabetes. By sticking to this guide, you can make informed choices that contribute to a healthier, more stable blood glucose profile. In the next chapters, we'll explore how to turn these ingredients into delicious, diabetes-friendly meals, complete with recipes and meal planning tips. This proactive approach to shopping and meal preparation is pivotal in taking control of your diabetes and living a healthier life.

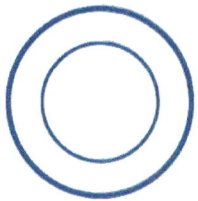 # BREAKFAST

★★★☆☆

🕐 **5 Minutes**   ♨🕐 **5 Minutes**   🍴 **1 servings**

## INGREDIENTS

- 1 slice of whole grain bread
- 1 ripe avocado
- 1 egg
- 1 tablespoon lime juice
- Salt and pepper to taste
- A pinch of chili flakes (optional)
- Fresh cilantro for garnish

## INSTRUCTIONS

1. Toast the bread to your desired level of crispiness using a toaster or oven.
2. Prepare the guacamole: In a small bowl, mash the ripe avocado with lime juice, salt, and pepper. You can add chili flakes for a bit of heat if desired.
3. Fry the egg: Heat a non-stick skillet over medium heat and carefully crack the egg into the pan, keeping the yolk intact. Fry until the edges are crispy and the yolk is still runny, about 3 minutes.
4. Assemble the toast: Spread the guacamole evenly over the toasted bread. Carefully place the fried egg on top.
5. Garnish and serve: Sprinkle fresh cilantro over the top and enjoy immediately.

# 1. Toast with Guacamole and Fried Egg

**Nutritional : Calories: 345 kcal | Protein: 11 g | Carbohydrates: 30 g | Fat: 21 g | Fiber: 9 g | Sugar: 3 g**

# 2.Spinach and Feta Egg Muffins

★★★☆☆

🕐 **10 Minutes**   ♨🕐 **25 Minutes**   🍴 **6 servings**

## INGREDIENTS

- 6 eggs
- 1/2 cup chopped fresh spinach
- 1/4 cup crumbled feta cheese
- 1/4 cup finely diced red bell pepper
- Salt and pepper to taste

## INSTRUCTIONS

1. Preheat the oven: Set the oven to 175 degrees Celsius (350 degrees Fahrenheit).
2. Prepare the egg mixture: In a bowl, beat the eggs and season with salt and pepper.
3. Add the vegetables and cheese: Mix in the chopped spinach, crumbled feta cheese, and diced red bell pepper.
4. Fill the muffin tin: Grease a muffin tin and evenly distribute the egg mixture among the muffin cups.
5. Bake: Place in the oven and bake for 25 minutes or until the muffins are set.
6. Serve: Let the muffins cool slightly before serving warm.

**Nutrition Facts (per muffin):Calories: 100 kcal | Protein: 7 g | Carbs: 2 g | Fat: 7 g | Fiber: 0.5 g | Sugar: 1 g**

★★★☆☆

🕐 15 Minutes | 🍳🕐 15 Minutes | 🍴 2 servings

## INGREDIENTS

- 1 cup rolled oats
- 1/2 cup Greek yogurt
- 1/2 cup almond milk
- 1 egg
- 1 teaspoon baking powder
- 1/2 teaspoon vanilla extract
- 1 banana, sliced
- 1 tablespoon chopped walnuts
- Fresh mint leaves for garnish (optional)

## INSTRUCTIONS

1. Blend the oats: Place the rolled oats in a blender and blend until they form a flour-like consistency.
2. Prepare the batter: In a bowl, mix the oat flour, Greek yogurt, almond milk, egg, baking powder, and vanilla extract until smooth.
3. Cook the pancakes: Heat a non-stick skillet over medium heat and pour small amounts of batter to form pancakes. Cook until bubbles form on the surface, then flip and cook until golden brown.
4. Serve: Stack the pancakes on a plate. Top with sliced banana, chopped walnuts, and a dollop of Greek yogurt.
5. Garnish: Add fresh mint leaves for an extra touch of freshness.

## 3. Toast with Guacamole and

**Nutritional : Calories: 300 kcal | Protein: 12 g | Carbs: 45 g | Fat: 8 g | Fiber: 6 g | Sugar: 10 g**

## 4.Overnight Oats with Blueberries and Almonds

★★★☆☆

🕐 10 Minutes | 🍳🕐 0 Minutes | 🍴 2 servings

## INGREDIENTS

- 1 cup rolled oats
- 1 cup unsweetened almond milk
- 1/2 cup Greek yogurt
- 1 tablespoon chia seeds
- 1/2 teaspoon vanilla extract
- 1 cup fresh blueberries
- 1/4 cup sliced almonds
- Drizzle of honey (optional)

## INSTRUCTIONS

1. Combine the ingredients: In a bowl, mix the rolled oats, almond milk, Greek yogurt, chia seeds, and vanilla extract until well combined.
2. Refrigerate overnight: Cover the bowl and refrigerate overnight, or for at least 4 hours, to allow the oats and chia seeds to absorb the liquid.
3. Serve: Stir the oats mixture before serving. Divide into two bowls.
4. Add toppings: Top each bowl with fresh blueberries, sliced almonds, and a drizzle of honey if desired.
5. Enjoy: Serve cold for a quick and nutritious breakfast.

**Nutrition Facts : Calories: 250 kcal | Protein: 10 g | Carbs: 35 g | Fat: 10 g | Fiber: 8 g | Sugar: 10 g**

# 5.Veggie-Packed Omelette

★★★☆☆

🕐 10 Minutes   🍳🕐 10 Minutes   🍴 1 servings

## INSTRUCTIONS

## INGREDIENTS

- 3 large eggs
- 1/4 cup diced red bell pepper
- 1/4 cup chopped spinach
- 1/4 cup diced tomatoes
- 1/4 cup chopped green onions
- 1/4 cup shredded mozzarella cheese
- Salt and pepper to taste
- 1 tablespoon olive oil
- Fresh basil leaves for garnish

**Nutrition Facts: Calories: 320 kcal | Protein: 20 g | Carbs: 8 g | Fat: 24 g | Fiber: 2 g | Sugar: 4 g**

# 6.Whole Wheat Waffles with Fresh Berries

★★★★☆

🕐 10 Minutes   🍳🕐 15 Minutes   🍴 4 servings

## INSTRUCTIONS

1. Preheat the waffle iron: Preheat your waffle iron according to the manufacturer's instructions.
2. Mix dry ingredients: In a large bowl, whisk together the whole wheat flour, sugar substitute, baking powder, and salt.
3. Combine wet ingredients: In another bowl, whisk together the almond milk, melted coconut oil, eggs, and vanilla extract.
4. Mix batter: Pour the wet ingredients into the dry ingredients and stir until just combined. Do not overmix.
5. Cook the waffles: Pour the batter onto the preheated waffle iron and cook according to the manufacturer's instructions until golden brown and crisp.
6. Serve: Serve the waffles warm, topped with fresh mixed berries and a drizzle of sugar-free berry syrup if desired. Garnish with fresh mint leaves for an extra touch of freshness.

## INGREDIENTS

- 1 1/2 cups whole wheat flour
- 2 tablespoons sugar substitute (like stevia)
- 1 tablespoon baking powder
- 1/2 teaspoon salt
- 1 3/4 cups unsweetened almond milk
- 1/4 cup melted coconut oil
- 2 large eggs
- 1 teaspoon vanilla extract
- Fresh mixed berries (strawberries, raspberries, blackberries)
- Sugar-free berry syrup (optional)
- Fresh mint leaves for garnish (optional)

**Nutrition Facts: Calories: 220 kcal | Protein: 8 g | Carbs: 30 g | Fat: 8 g | Fiber: 6 g | Sugar: 5 g**

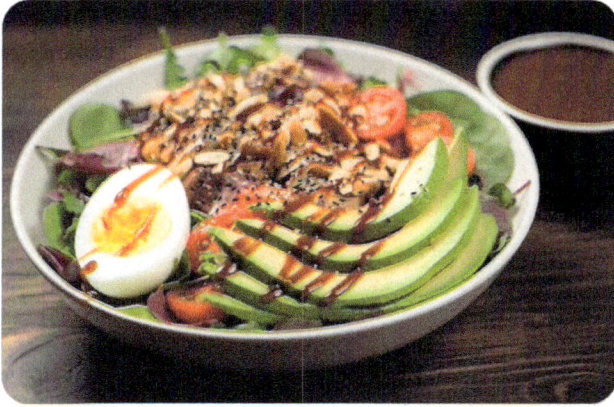

# 7.Avocado and Egg Breakfast Salad

★★★☆☆

🕐 10 Minutes   🍳🕐 10 Minutes   🍴 2 servings

## INGREDIENTS

- 4 cups mixed salad greens (spinach, arugula, etc.)
- 1 ripe avocado, sliced
- 2 hard-boiled eggs, halved
- 1 cup cherry tomatoes, halved
- 1/4 cup sliced almonds or peanuts
- 1 tablespoon sesame seeds
- 2 tablespoons balsamic glaze or sugar-free dressing
- Salt and pepper to taste

## INSTRUCTIONS

1. Prepare the eggs: Hard-boil the eggs by placing them in a pot of boiling water for about 10 minutes. Once cooked, cool, peel, and halve them.
2. Assemble the salad: In a large bowl or two individual bowls, place the mixed salad greens as the base.
3. Add the toppings: Arrange the avocado slices, hard-boiled egg halves, and cherry tomato halves on top of the greens.
4. Add nuts and seeds: Sprinkle the sliced almonds or peanuts and sesame seeds over the salad.
5. Season: Drizzle with balsamic glaze or your choice of sugar-free dressing. Season with salt and pepper to taste.
6. Serve: Enjoy immediately for a fresh, nutritious breakfast.

**Nutrition Facts : Calories: 350 kcal | Protein: 12 g | Carbs: 18 g | Fat: 28 g | Fiber: 10 g | Sugar: 6 g**

# 8.Mushroom and Herb Frittata

★★★★☆

🕐 10 Minutes   🍳🕐 20 Minutes   🍴 4 servings

## INSTRUCTIONS

1. Preheat the oven: Preheat your oven to 175 degrees Celsius (350 degrees Fahrenheit).
2. Sauté the vegetables: In an oven-safe skillet, heat the olive oil over medium heat. Add the chopped onion and cook until translucent, about 3 minutes. Add the sliced mushrooms and cook until they are tender and any liquid has evaporated, about 5 minutes.
3. Prepare the egg mixture: In a large bowl, whisk together the eggs, milk, chopped herbs, salt, and pepper.
4. Combine and cook: Pour the egg mixture over the sautéed vegetables in the skillet. Stir gently to distribute the vegetables evenly. Cook for about 2-3 minutes, or until the edges start to set.
5. Add the cheese and bake: Sprinkle the shredded cheese evenly over the top of the frittata. Transfer the skillet to the preheated oven and bake for 15 minutes, or until the frittata is fully set and the top is golden brown.
6. Serve: Remove from the oven and let cool for a few minutes before slicing. Serve warm, garnished with additional fresh herbs if desired.

## INGREDIENTS

- 8 large eggs
- 1/2 cup milk (dairy or non-dairy)
- 1 cup sliced mushrooms (button, cremini, or your choice)
- 1/4 cup chopped fresh herbs (such as thyme, rosemary, and parsley)
- 1/2 cup shredded mozzarella or cheddar cheese
- 1/2 small onion, finely chopped
- 2 tablespoons olive oil
- Salt and pepper to taste

**Nutrition Facts: Calories: 220 kcal | Protein: 14 g | Carbs: 4 g | Fat: 16 g | Fiber: 1 g | Sugar: 2 g**

# 7.Avocado and Egg Breakfast Salad

★★★★★

🕐 10 Minutes   🍳 0 Minutes   🍴 1 servings

## INSTRUCTIONS

1. Toast the bread: Toast the slices of whole grain bread to your desired level of crispness.
2. Prepare the avocado: Cut the avocado in half, remove the pit, and scoop out the flesh into a bowl. Mash the avocado with a fork until smooth. Season with salt and pepper to taste.
3. Assemble the toast: Spread the mashed avocado evenly on the toasted bread slices.
4. Add the toppings: Top each slice with halved cherry tomatoes and chopped basil leaves.
5. Drizzle with olive oil: Drizzle a small amount of olive oil over the tomatoes.
6. Season: Add a pinch of red pepper flakes if you like a bit of heat.
7. Serve: Serve immediately and enjoy your fresh and nutritious avocado toast.

## INGREDIENTS

- 2 slices whole grain bread
- 1 ripe avocado
- 1 cup cherry tomatoes, halved
- 1 tablespoon fresh basil leaves, chopped
- Salt and pepper to taste
- 1 teaspoon olive oil
- Red pepper flakes (optional)

**Nutrition Facts : Calories: 250 kcal | Protein: 6 g | Carbs: 30 g | Fat: 14 g | Fiber: 10 g | Sugar: 3 g**

# 10.Hummus with Fresh Veggie Sticks

★★★★★

🕐 10 Minutes   🍳 15 Minutes   🍴 4 servings

## INSTRUCTIONS

1. Blend the hummus: In a food processor, combine the tahini and lemon juice. Process for about 1 minute until smooth and creamy. Scrape the sides and bottom of the bowl then process for another 30 seconds.
2. Add the remaining ingredients: Add the olive oil, minced garlic, cumin, and a pinch of salt to the whipped tahini and lemon juice. Process for 30 seconds, scrape the sides and bottom of the bowl, and then process another 30 seconds or until well blended.
3. Add the chickpeas: Add half of the chickpeas to the food processor and process for 1 minute. Scrape sides and bottom of the bowl, then add remaining chickpeas and process until thick and quite smooth, 1 to 2 minutes.
4. Adjust consistency: With the food processor running, add 2 to 3 tablespoons of water until you reach your desired consistency.
5. Serve: Transfer the hummus to a serving bowl, drizzle with a bit of olive oil, and sprinkle with chopped parsley.
6. Prepare the veggies: Arrange the carrot sticks, celery sticks, cucumber slices, and red bell pepper slices around the hummus bowl.
7. Enjoy: Serve immediately or refrigerate for up to a week.

## INGREDIENTS

- 1 can (15 oz) chickpeas, drained and rinsed
- 1/4 cup fresh lemon juice (1 large lemon)
- 1/4 cup well-stirred tahini
- 1 small garlic clove, minced
- 2 tablespoons extra-virgin olive oil, plus more for serving
- 1/2 teaspoon ground cumin
- Salt to taste
- 2-3 tablespoons water
- Fresh parsley, chopped (for garnish)
- Veggies for Dipping:
- 2 large carrots, peeled and cut into sticks
- 2 large celery stalks, cut into sticks
- 1 cucumber, sliced
- 1 red bell pepper, sliced

**Nutrition Facts: Calories: 180 kcal | Protein: 6 g | Carbs: 18 g | Fat: 9 g | Fiber: 6 g | Sugar: 4 g**

# 11.Blueberry Mint Smoothie

★★★☆☆

🕐 10 Minutes  |  ♨🕐 0 Minutes  |  🍴 2 servings

## INGREDIENTS

- 1 cup fresh or frozen blueberries
- 1 banana, sliced
- 1/2 cup Greek yogurt
- 1/2 cup unsweetened almond milk
- 1 tablespoon chia seeds
- 1 tablespoon honey (optional)
- Fresh mint leaves (for garnish)
- Ice cubes (optional)

## INSTRUCTIONS

1. Prepare the ingredients: If using fresh blueberries, rinse them thoroughly. Slice the banana.
2. Blend the smoothie: In a blender, combine the blueberries, banana, Greek yogurt, almond milk, chia seeds, and honey (if using). Blend until smooth and creamy. If you prefer a thicker smoothie, add a few ice cubes and blend again.
3. Serve: Pour the smoothie into two glasses.
4. Garnish: Garnish with fresh mint leaves and a few extra blueberries on top.
5. Enjoy: Serve immediately for a refreshing and nutritious start to your day.

**Nutrition Facts: Calories: 180 kcal | Protein: 6 g | Carbs: 30 g | Fat: 3 g | Fiber: 6 g | Sugar: 20 g**

# 12.Grilled Salmon Fillet with Lemon

★★★★☆

🕐 10 Minutes  |  ♨🕐 25 Minutes  |  🍴 4 servings

## INGREDIENTS

- 6 large eggs
- 1/4 cup milk (dairy or non-dairy)
- 1 cup broccoli florets, chopped
- 1/2 cup shredded cheddar cheese
- 1/4 cup grated Parmesan cheese
- 1 small onion, finely chopped
- 2 tablespoons olive oil
- Salt and pepper to taste
- Fresh chives, chopped (for garnish)

## INSTRUCTIONS

1. Preheat the oven: Preheat your oven to 175 degrees Celsius (350 degrees Fahrenheit).
2. Sauté the vegetables: In an oven-safe skillet, heat the olive oil over medium heat. Add the chopped onion and cook until translucent, about 3 minutes. Add the chopped broccoli florets and cook for an additional 5 minutes until tender.
3. Prepare the egg mixture: In a large bowl, whisk together the eggs, milk, salt, and pepper. Stir in the shredded cheddar cheese and grated Parmesan cheese.
4. Combine and cook: Pour the egg mixture over the sautéed vegetables in the skillet. Stir gently to distribute the vegetables evenly. Cook for about 2-3 minutes, or until the edges start to set.
5. Bake: Transfer the skillet to the preheated oven and bake for 15 minutes, or until the frittata is fully set and the top is golden brown.
6. Serve: Remove from the oven and let cool for a few minutes before slicing. Garnish with chopped fresh chives and serve warm.

**Nutrition Facts: Calories: 220 kcal | Protein: 15 g | Carbs: 6 g | Fat: 16 g | Fiber: 2 g | Sugar: 2 g**

# 13.Stacked Pancakes with Berries

★★★☆☆

🕐 10 Minutes  |  🍳🕐 0 Minutes  |  🍴 2 servings

## INGREDIENTS

- 1 cup whole wheat flour
- 1 teaspoon baking powder
- 1 cup milk
- 1 egg
- 1 tablespoon honey
- 1/2 teaspoon vanilla extract
- 1 cup mixed berries (strawberries, blueberries, raspberries)
- Maple syrup (for serving)

## INSTRUCTIONS

1. Combine the whole wheat flour and baking powder in a large mixing bowl.
2. In another bowl, whisk together the milk, egg, honey, and vanilla extract.
3. Pour the wet ingredients into the dry ingredients and stir until just combined.
4. Heat a non-stick skillet over medium heat and pour 1/4 cup of batter for each pancake. Cook until bubbles form on the surface, then flip and cook until golden brown on both sides.
5. Serve the pancakes stacked high with fresh berries on top and a drizzle of maple syrup.

**Nutritional: Calories: 375 kcal | Protein: 12 g | Carbohydrates: 65 g | Fat: 8 g | Fiber: 8 g | Sugar: 18 g**

# 14.Oatmeal Served with Yogurt and Fresh Fruit

★★★★☆

🕐 5 Minutes  |  🍳🕐 10 Minutes  |  🍴 1 servings

## INGREDIENTS

- 1/2 cup rolled oats
- 1 cup water or milk
- Pinch of salt
- 1/2 cup Greek yogurt
- 1/2 cup mixed fresh fruit (such as berries, sliced banana, or diced apple)
- 1 tablespoon honey (optional)

## INSTRUCTIONS

1. Bring the water or milk to a boil in a small saucepan. Add the oats and a pinch of salt, then reduce the heat to low.
2. Simmer uncovered for 10 minutes, stirring occasionally, until the oats are soft and have absorbed most of the liquid.
3. Transfer the cooked oats to a bowl and let cool slightly.
4. Top with Greek yogurt and fresh fruit.
5. Drizzle with honey if desired and serve immediately.

**Nutritional: Calories: 350 kcal | Protein: 15 g | Carbohydrates: 55 g | Fat: 7 g | Fiber: 6 g | Sugar: 18 g**

# 15. Greek Yogurt and Spiced Apples

★★★☆☆

🕐 **5 Minutes**    ⏲ **10 Minutes**    🍴 **1 servings**

## INGREDIENTS

- 1 cup Greek yogurt
- 1 apple, cored and sliced
- 1 tablespoon honey
- 1/2 teaspoon ground cinnamon
- 1/4 teaspoon ground nutmeg
- A handful of walnuts, chopped

## INSTRUCTIONS

1. In a small skillet, combine the sliced apple, honey, cinnamon, and nutmeg. Cook over medium heat until the apples are soft and caramelized, about 10 minutes.
2. Place Greek yogurt in a serving bowl.
3. Top with the spiced apple mixture and sprinkle with chopped walnuts.
4. Serve immediately for a warm, comforting breakfast.

**Nutritional : Calories: 290 kcal | Protein: 15 g | Carbohydrates: 42 g | Fat: 8 g | Fiber: 5 g | Sugar: 32 g**

# 16. Quinoa and Black Bean Salad with Avocado and Lime

★★★★☆

🕐 **15 Minutes**    ⏲ **15 Minutes**    🍴 **4 servings**

## INGREDIENTS

- 1 cup quinoa, rinsed
- 2 cups water
- 1 can (15 oz) black beans, drained and rinsed
- 1 avocado, sliced
- 1 cup cherry tomatoes, halved
- 1/4 cup red onion, finely chopped
- 1/4 cup fresh cilantro, chopped
- 2 tablespoons olive oil
- Juice of 1 lime
- Salt and pepper to taste

## INSTRUCTIONS

1. Cook the quinoa: In a medium saucepan, bring the quinoa and water to a boil. Reduce heat to low, cover, and simmer for about 15 minutes, or until the quinoa is tender and the water is absorbed. Remove from heat and let it cool.
2. Prepare the salad: In a large bowl, combine the cooked quinoa, black beans, cherry tomatoes, red onion, and fresh cilantro.
3. Make the dressing: In a small bowl, whisk together the olive oil, lime juice, salt, and pepper.
4. Combine and serve: Pour the dressing over the quinoa mixture and toss to combine. Gently fold in the avocado slices. Serve over mixed greens if desired.
5. Garnish: Garnish with extra cilantro and lime wedges if desired.

**Nutrition Facts: Calories: 320 kcal | Protein: 10 g | Carbs: 38 g | Fat: 15 g | Fiber: 12 g | Sugar: 3 g**

# GRAINS, LEGUME

# 17. White Bean and Kale Stew

★★★☆☆

🕐 **15 Minutes**   ♨🕐 **30 Minutes**   🍴 **4 servings**

## INGREDIENTS

- 1 tablespoon olive oil
- 1 onion, finely chopped
- 2 garlic cloves, minced
- 2 celery stalks, diced
- 2 carrots, diced
- 1 can (15 oz) white beans, drained and rinsed
- 4 cups vegetable broth
- 4 cups chopped kale
- 1 teaspoon dried thyme
- 1 teaspoon dried rosemary
- Salt and pepper to taste
- 1 tablespoon chopped fresh parsley (for garnish)
- Red pepper flakes (optional)

## INSTRUCTIONS

1. Sauté the aromatics: In a large pot, heat the olive oil over medium heat. Add the chopped onion, garlic, celery, and carrots. Sauté for about 5 minutes until the vegetables are softened.
2. Add the beans and broth: Stir in the white beans, vegetable broth, dried thyme, and dried rosemary. Bring the mixture to a boil.
3. Simmer the stew: Reduce the heat to low and let it simmer for about 20 minutes, allowing the flavors to meld together.
4. Add the kale: Stir in the chopped kale and continue to simmer for another 5-10 minutes until the kale is tender.
5. Season: Taste and season with salt, pepper, and red pepper flakes (if using).
6. Serve: Ladle the stew into bowls and garnish with fresh parsley. Serve hot.

**Nutrition Facts:bCalories: 180 kcal | Protein: 8 g | Carbs: 30 g | Fat: 4 g | Fiber: 10 g | Sugar: 6 g**

# 18. Brown Rice and Vegetable Stir-Fry with Tofu

★★★★☆

🕐 **15 Minutes**   ♨🕐 **20 Minutes**   🍴 **4 servings**

## INGREDIENTS

- 1 cup brown rice
- 2 cups water
- 1 block (14 oz) firm tofu, pressed and cubed
- 2 tablespoons soy sauce (low-sodium)
- 1 tablespoon sesame oil
- 2 cups broccoli florets
- 1 red bell pepper, sliced
- 1 small red onion, thinly sliced
- 2 garlic cloves, minced
- 1 tablespoon grated fresh ginger
- 2 green onions, sliced
- 1 tablespoon olive oil
- Salt and pepper to taste

## INSTRUCTIONS

1. Cook the brown rice: In a medium saucepan, bring the brown rice and water to a boil. Reduce heat to low, cover, and simmer for about 40 minutes, or until the rice is tender and the water is absorbed. Fluff with a fork and set aside.
2. Prepare the tofu: While the rice is cooking, press the tofu to remove excess moisture. Cut the tofu into cubes and toss with 1 tablespoon of soy sauce.
3. Cook the tofu: In a large skillet or wok, heat the sesame oil over medium-high heat. Add the tofu and cook until golden brown on all sides, about 5-7 minutes. Remove from the skillet and set aside.
4. Stir-fry the vegetables: In the same skillet, heat the olive oil over medium-high heat. Add the garlic and ginger and sauté for about 1 minute until fragrant. Add the broccoli florets, red bell pepper, and red onion. Stir-fry for about 5-7 minutes until the vegetables are tender-crisp.
5. Combine and season: Add the cooked brown rice and tofu back to the skillet with the vegetables. Drizzle with the remaining soy sauce and toss to combine. Cook for an additional 2-3 minutes to heat through. Season with salt and pepper to taste.
6. Serve: Garnish with sliced green onions and serve immediately.

**Nutrition Facts: Calories: 320 kcal | Protein: 12 g | Carbs: 40 g | Fat: 12 g | Fiber: 6 g | Sugar: 4 g**

# 19.Quinoa Tabbouleh Salad

★★★☆☆

🕐 15 Minutes  🍳🕐 15 Minutes  🍴 4 servings

## INGREDIENTS

- 1 cup quinoa, rinsed
- 2 cups water
- 1 cup chopped fresh parsley
- 1/2 cup chopped fresh mint
- 1 cup diced tomatoes
- 1 cucumber, diced
- 1/4 cup finely chopped red onion
- 1/4 cup lemon juice (about 2 lemons)
- 3 tablespoons olive oil
- Salt and pepper to taste

## INSTRUCTIONS

1. Cook the quinoa: In a medium saucepan, bring the quinoa and water to a boil. Reduce heat to low, cover, and simmer for about 15 minutes, or until the quinoa is tender and the water is absorbed. Remove from heat and let it cool.
2. Prepare the vegetables: While the quinoa is cooling, chop the parsley, mint, tomatoes, cucumber, and red onion. Place them in a large bowl.
3. Combine ingredients: Add the cooled quinoa to the bowl with the vegetables.
4. Make the dressing: In a small bowl, whisk together the lemon juice, olive oil, salt, and pepper.
5. Mix the salad: Pour the dressing over the quinoa and vegetables. Toss well to combine.
6. Serve: Serve immediately or refrigerate for an hour to let the flavors meld together.

**Nutrition Facts: Calories: 200 kcal | Protein: 6 g | Carbs: 28 g | Fat: 8 g | Fiber: 4 g | Sugar: 3 g**

# 20.Three-Bean Vegetable Stew

★★★★☆

🕐 15 Minutes  🍳🕐 30 Minutes  🍴 4 servings

## INGREDIENTS

- 1 tablespoon olive oil
- 1 onion, finely chopped
- 2 garlic cloves, minced
- 1 red bell pepper, diced
- 1 carrot, diced
- 1 zucchini, diced
- 1 can (15 oz) kidney beans, drained and rinsed
- 1 can (15 oz) cannellini beans, drained and rinsed
- 1 can (15 oz) chickpeas, drained and rinsed
- 1 cup frozen peas
- 1 can (14.5 oz) diced tomatoes
- 4 cups vegetable broth
- 1 teaspoon ground cumin
- 1 teaspoon smoked paprika
- Salt and pepper to taste
- Fresh cilantro, chopped (for garnish)

## INSTRUCTIONS

1. Sauté the aromatics: In a large pot, heat the olive oil over medium heat. Add the chopped onion and garlic and sauté for about 3 minutes until translucent.
2. Add the vegetables: Add the diced red bell pepper, carrot, and zucchini to the pot. Sauté for an additional 5 minutes until the vegetables begin to soften.
3. Add the beans and spices: Stir in the kidney beans, cannellini beans, chickpeas, and frozen peas. Add the diced tomatoes, vegetable broth, ground cumin, and smoked paprika. Season with salt and pepper to taste.
4. Simmer the stew: Bring the mixture to a boil, then reduce the heat and let it simmer for about 20 minutes, or until the vegetables are tender and the flavors have melded together.
5. Serve: Ladle the stew into bowls and garnish with fresh cilantro. Serve hot.

**Nutrition Facts: Calories: 280 kcal | Protein: 12 g | Carbs: 45 g | Fat: 6 g | Fiber: 14 g | Sugar: 8 g**

# 21.Fresh Tomato and Onion Salad

★★★☆☆

🕐 10 Minutes   🍲🕐 0 Minutes   🍴 4 servings

## INGREDIENTS

- 4 large tomatoes, sliced
- 1 red onion, thinly sliced
- 1/4 cup fresh parsley, chopped
- 2 tablespoons olive oil
- 1 tablespoon red wine vinegar
- Salt and pepper to taste
- 1 teaspoon dried oregano
- Fresh basil leaves (for garnish)

## INSTRUCTIONS

1. Prepare the vegetables: Slice the tomatoes and red onion. Chop the fresh parsley.
2. Assemble the salad: Arrange the tomato slices and red onion rings on a large serving plate. Sprinkle the chopped parsley over the top.
3. Make the dressing: In a small bowl, whisk together the olive oil, red wine vinegar, salt, pepper, and dried oregano.
4. Dress the salad: Drizzle the dressing evenly over the tomato and onion slices.
5. Garnish and serve: Garnish with fresh basil leaves and serve immediately.

**Nutrition Facts: Calories: 90 kcal | Protein: 1 g | Carbs: 6 g | Fat: 7 g | Fiber: 2 g | Sugar: 4 g**

# 22.Spiced Pumpkin Soup

★★★★☆

🕐 15 Minutes   🍲🕐 30 Minutes   🍴 4 servings

## INGREDIENTS

- 1 medium pumpkin (about 2 pounds), peeled, seeded, and cubed
- 1 tablespoon olive oil
- 1 onion, chopped
- 2 garlic cloves, minced
- 1 teaspoon ground cumin
- 1/2 teaspoon ground ginger
- 1/2 teaspoon ground cinnamon
- 1/4 teaspoon ground nutmeg
- 4 cups low-sodium vegetable broth
- 1/2 cup coconut milk
- Salt and pepper to taste
- Fresh basil leaves for garnish
- Red pepper flakes for garnish (optional)

## INSTRUCTIONS

1. Prepare the pumpkin: Peel, seed, and cube the pumpkin. Set aside.
2. Sauté the aromatics: In a large pot, heat the olive oil over medium heat. Add the chopped onion and sauté until translucent, about 5 minutes. Add the minced garlic and cook for another minute.
3. Add spices and pumpkin: Stir in the ground cumin, ground ginger, ground cinnamon, and ground nutmeg. Cook for about 1 minute until fragrant. Add the cubed pumpkin to the pot and stir to coat with the spices.
4. Add broth and simmer: Pour in the vegetable broth and bring the mixture to a boil. Reduce heat and let it simmer for about 20 minutes, or until the pumpkin is tender.
5. Blend the soup: Use an immersion blender to puree the soup until smooth. Alternatively, you can transfer the soup to a blender and puree it in batches.
6. Finish the soup: Stir in the coconut milk and season with salt and pepper to taste. Heat through but do not boil.
7. Serve: Ladle the soup into bowls and garnish with fresh basil leaves and red pepper flakes if desired.

**Nutrition Facts: Calories: 180 kcal | Protein: 3 g | Carbs: 25 g | Fat: 8 g | Fiber: 5 g | Sugar: 8 g**

# 23.Spring Vegetable Ribollita

★★★★★

🕐 20 Minutes | 🍳🕐 40 Minutes | 🍴 4 servings

## INGREDIENTS

- 2 tablespoons olive oil
- 1 onion, finely chopped
- 2 garlic cloves, minced
- 2 celery stalks, diced
- 2 carrots, diced
- 1 zucchini, diced
- 1 cup fresh or frozen peas
- 1 cup chopped kale or spinach
- 1 can (15 oz) cannellini beans, drained and rinsed
- 4 cups low-sodium vegetable broth
- 1 cup diced tomatoes (fresh or canned)
- 1 teaspoon dried thyme
- 1 teaspoon dried oregano
- Salt and pepper to taste
- Fresh parsley, chopped (for garnish)

## INSTRUCTIONS

1. Sauté the aromatics: In a large pot, heat the olive oil over medium heat. Add the chopped onion and sauté until translucent, about 5 minutes. Add the minced garlic and cook for another minute.
2. Add the vegetables: Add the diced celery, carrots, and zucchini to the pot. Cook for about 5 minutes until the vegetables start to soften.
3. Add the greens and peas: Stir in the chopped kale or spinach and fresh or frozen peas. Cook for another 3-4 minutes.
4. Add the beans and broth: Stir in the cannellini beans, vegetable broth, and diced tomatoes. Add the dried thyme and oregano. Season with salt and pepper to taste.
5. Simmer the stew: Bring the mixture to a boil, then reduce the heat and let it simmer for about 20-25 minutes until all the vegetables are tender and the flavors have melded together.
6. Serve: Ladle the ribollita into bowls and garnish with fresh chopped parsley. Serve hot.

**Nutrition Facts: Calories: 220 kcal | Protein: 8 g | Carbs: 32 g | Fat: 7 g | Fiber: 10 g | Sugar: 8 g**

# 24.Black Bean and Veggie Burrito

★★★★☆

🕐 15 Minutes | 🍳🕐 10 Minutes | 🍴 4 servings

## INGREDIENTS

- 1 tablespoon olive oil
- 1 small onion, diced
- 2 garlic cloves, minced
- 1 red bell pepper, diced
- 1 zucchini, diced
- 1 can (15 oz) black beans, drained and rinsed
- 1 teaspoon ground cumin
- 1 teaspoon chili powder
- Salt and pepper to taste
- 1/4 cup fresh cilantro, chopped
- 1 avocado, diced
- 1/2 cup salsa
- 4 whole wheat tortillas
- Fresh lime wedges (for serving)

## INSTRUCTIONS

1. Sauté the aromatics: In a large skillet, heat the olive oil over medium heat. Add the diced onion and sauté until translucent, about 5 minutes. Add the minced garlic and cook for another minute.
2. Cook the vegetables: Add the diced red bell pepper and zucchini to the skillet. Cook for about 5 minutes until the vegetables are tender.
3. Add the beans and spices: Stir in the black beans, ground cumin, and chili powder. Season with salt and pepper to taste. Cook for an additional 2-3 minutes until the beans are heated through. Remove from heat and stir in the chopped cilantro.
4. Prepare the burritos: Lay each tortilla flat and spoon an equal amount of the bean and vegetable mixture onto each tortilla. Top with diced avocado and salsa.
5. Wrap the burritos: Fold in the sides of the tortilla and then roll it up from the bottom to the top. Serve immediately with fresh lime wedges.

**Nutrition Facts: Calories: 350 kcal | Protein: 12 g | Carbs: 48 g | Fat: 12 g | Fiber: 14 g | Sugar: 4 g**

# 25.Mediterranean Chickpea Salad with Feta and Olives

★★★☆☆

🕐 10 Minutes   🍳🕐 0 Minutes   🍴 4 servings

## INGREDIENTS

- 2 cans (15 oz each) chickpeas, rinsed and drained
- 1 cup cherry tomatoes, halved
- 1/2 cup Kalamata olives, pitted and sliced
- 1/2 red onion, thinly sliced
- 1/2 cup feta cheese, crumbled
- 1/4 cup fresh parsley, chopped
- 1/4 cup olive oil
- 2 tablespoons lemon juice
- 1 teaspoon dried oregano
- Salt and pepper to taste
- Instructions:

## INSTRUCTIONS

1. In a large bowl, combine chickpeas, cherry tomatoes, olives, red onion, and feta cheese.
2. In a small bowl, whisk together olive oil, lemon juice, oregano, salt, and pepper.
3. Pour the dressing over the salad and toss to combine.
4. Garnish with fresh parsley before serving.
5. Serve chilled or at room temperature for best flavor.

**Nutritional: Calories: 345 kcal | Protein: 12 g | Carbohydrates: 30 g | Fat: 20 g | Fiber: 8 g | Sugar: 5 g**

# 26.Lentil Soup with Carrots, Celery, and Spinach

★★★★☆

🕐 10 Minutes   🍳🕐 40 Minutes   🍴 4 servings

## INGREDIENTS

- 1 cup dried lentils, rinsed
- 1 tablespoon olive oil
- 1 onion, chopped
- 2 carrots, diced
- 2 celery stalks, diced
- 3 cloves garlic, minced
- 6 cups vegetable broth
- 2 cups fresh spinach leaves
- Salt and pepper to taste
- 1 teaspoon dried thyme

## INSTRUCTIONS

1. Heat olive oil in a large pot over medium heat. Add onion, carrots, celery, and garlic. Cook until vegetables are softened, about 10 minutes.
2. Add lentils, vegetable broth, and thyme. Bring to a boil, then reduce heat and simmer for 30 minutes, or until lentils are tender.
3. Stir in spinach and cook until wilted, about 5 minutes.
4. Season with salt and pepper.
5. Serve hot, with crusty bread if desired.

**Nutritional: Calories: 240 kcal | Protein: 14 g | Carbohydrates: 35 g | Fat: 5 g | Fiber: 15 g | Sugar: 6 g**

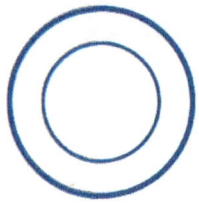

# SIDES AND VEGETABLE

## 27. Grilled Zucchini Ribbons with Fresh Herbs

★★★☆☆

🕐 10 Minutes          ♨🕐 10 Minutes          🍴 4 servings

### INGREDIENTS

- 4 medium zucchinis, sliced into thin ribbons
- 2 tablespoons olive oil
- 1 teaspoon garlic powder
- Salt and pepper to taste
- 1/4 cup fresh mint leaves, chopped
- 1/4 cup fresh basil leaves, chopped
- Lemon wedges for serving

### INSTRUCTIONS

1. Prepare the zucchini: Slice the zucchinis into thin ribbons using a mandoline or vegetable peeler.
2. Season the zucchini: In a large bowl, toss the zucchini ribbons with olive oil, garlic powder, salt, and pepper until well coated.
3. Grill the zucchini: Preheat the grill to medium-high heat. Place the zucchini ribbons on the grill and cook for about 2-3 minutes on each side, or until they are tender and have nice grill marks.
4. Add fresh herbs: Remove the grilled zucchini ribbons from the grill and place them on a serving platter. Sprinkle with chopped mint and basil leaves.
5. Serve: Serve immediately with lemon wedges on the side for squeezing over the zucchini ribbons.

Nutritional: Calories: 85 kcal | Protein: 2 g | Carbohydrates: 5 g | Fat: 7 g | Fiber: 2 g | Sugar: 3 g

## 28. Avocado, Tomato, and Feta Salad

★★★★☆

🕐 10 Minutes          ♨🕐 0 Minutes          🍴 4 servings

### INGREDIENTS

- 2 ripe avocados, sliced
- 1 cup cherry tomatoes, halved
- 1/2 cup feta cheese, crumbled
- 1/4 cup fresh basil leaves
- 2 tablespoons olive oil
- 1 tablespoon lemon juice
- Salt and pepper to taste

### INSTRUCTIONS

1. Prepare the ingredients: Slice the avocados and halve the cherry tomatoes. Crumble the feta cheese and wash the basil leaves.
2. Combine the salad: In a large bowl, gently combine the avocado slices, cherry tomatoes, and crumbled feta cheese.
3. Make the dressing: In a small bowl, whisk together the olive oil, lemon juice, salt, and pepper.
4. Dress the salad: Pour the dressing over the salad and gently toss to coat.
5. Serve: Garnish with fresh basil leaves and serve immediately.

Nutritional: Calories: 285 kcal | Protein: 6 g | Carbohydrates: 12 g | Fat: 24 g | Fiber: 7 g | Sugar: 2 g

## 29.Fresh Tomato, Cucumber, and Lettuce Salad with Flax Seeds

★★★☆☆

🕐 10 Minutes  |  ♨🕐 10 Minutes  |  🍴 4 servings

### INGREDIENTS

- 2 cups lettuce leaves, torn
- 1 cup cherry tomatoes, halved
- 1 cup cucumber, sliced
- 1 tablespoon flax seeds
- 2 tablespoons olive oil
- 1 tablespoon apple cider vinegar
- Salt and pepper to taste

### INSTRUCTIONS

1. Prepare the vegetables: Wash and dry the lettuce leaves, then tear them into bite-sized pieces. Halve the cherry tomatoes and slice the cucumber.
2. Combine the salad: In a large bowl, combine the lettuce, cherry tomatoes, and cucumber.
3. Make the dressing: In a small bowl, whisk together the olive oil, apple cider vinegar, salt, and pepper.
4. Dress the salad: Pour the dressing over the salad and toss gently to coat.
5. Garnish: Sprinkle the flax seeds over the top of the salad.
6. Serve: Serve immediately for the freshest flavor.

Nutritional: Calories: 105 kcal | Protein: 2 g | Carbohydrates: 7 g | Fat: 8 g | Fiber: 3 g | Sugar: 3 g

## 30.Balsamic Roasted Brussels Sprouts

★★★★☆

🕐 10 Minutes  |  ♨🕐 30 Minutes  |  🍴 4 servings

### INGREDIENTS

- 1 pound Brussels sprouts, trimmed and halved
- 2 tablespoons olive oil
- 2 tablespoons balsamic vinegar
- 1 tablespoon honey or sugar-free maple syrup
- 1 teaspoon fresh thyme, chopped
- Salt and pepper to taste

### INSTRUCTIONS

1. Preheat Oven: Preheat your oven to 200°C (400°F).
2. Prepare Brussels Sprouts: In a large bowl, toss the Brussels sprouts with olive oil, salt, and pepper until evenly coated.
3. Roast: Spread the Brussels sprouts in a single layer on a baking sheet. Roast in the preheated oven for 25-30 minutes, stirring halfway through, until the sprouts are tender and caramelized.
4. Make the Glaze: While the Brussels sprouts are roasting, combine the balsamic vinegar and honey (or sugar-free maple syrup) in a small saucepan. Bring to a simmer over medium heat and cook until the mixture has reduced by half and is syrupy, about 5-7 minutes.
5. Toss and Serve: Drizzle the balsamic glaze over the roasted Brussels sprouts and toss to coat evenly. Garnish with fresh thyme before serving

Nutritional: Calories: 120 kcal | Protein: 3 g | Carbohydrates: 12 g | Fat: 7 g | Fiber: 4 g | Sugar: 6 g

# 31.Spicy Baked Cauliflower Bites

★★★☆☆

🕐 15 Minutes   ♨🕐 30 Minutes   🍴 4 servings

## INGREDIENTS

- 1 large head cauliflower, cut into florets
- 2 tablespoons olive oil
- 1/2 cup hot sauce (like Frank's RedHot)
- 1 tablespoon apple cider vinegar
- 1 teaspoon garlic powder
- 1 teaspoon paprika
- 1/2 teaspoon cayenne pepper (optional, for extra heat)
- Salt and pepper to taste
- Fresh parsley, chopped (for garnish)

## INSTRUCTIONS

1. Preheat Oven: Preheat your oven to 200°C (400°F). Line a baking sheet with parchment paper.
2. Prepare Cauliflower: In a large bowl, toss the cauliflower florets with olive oil, garlic powder, paprika, cayenne pepper (if using), salt, and pepper until evenly coated.
3. Bake: Spread the cauliflower florets in a single layer on the prepared baking sheet. Bake in the preheated oven for 20 minutes, flipping halfway through.
4. Prepare Sauce: In a small bowl, mix the hot sauce and apple cider vinegar.
5. Coat Cauliflower: After 20 minutes, remove the cauliflower from the oven and pour the hot sauce mixture over the florets. Toss to coat evenly.
6. Bake Again: Return the cauliflower to the oven and bake for an additional 10 minutes, or until the cauliflower is tender and slightly crispy.
7. Serve: Garnish with fresh parsley and serve with your favorite dipping sauce, like a low-fat yogurt dip or a homemade ranch.

**Nutritional: Calories: 120 kcal | Protein: 3 g | Carbohydrates: 10 g | Fat: 8 g | Fiber: 4 g | Sugar: 2 g**

# 32.Lemon Garlic Roasted Asparagus

★★★★☆

🕐 10 Minutes   ♨🕐 15 Minutes   🍴 4 servings

## INGREDIENTS

- 1 bunch asparagus, trimmed
- 2 tablespoons olive oil
- 2 cloves garlic, minced
- 1 lemon, zested and juiced
- Salt and pepper to taste
- Fresh parsley, chopped (for garnish)

## INSTRUCTIONS

1. Preheat Oven: Preheat your oven to 200°C (400°F). Line a baking sheet with parchment paper.
2. Prepare Asparagus: Spread the trimmed asparagus on the prepared baking sheet.
3. Season: Drizzle with olive oil, sprinkle with minced garlic, lemon zest, salt, and pepper. Toss to coat evenly.
4. Roast: Roast in the preheated oven for 12-15 minutes, or until the asparagus is tender and lightly browned.
5. Serve: Remove from the oven, drizzle with fresh lemon juice, and garnish with chopped parsley. Serve hot.

**Nutritional: Calories: 90 kcal | Protein: 2 g | Carbohydrates: 5 g | Fat: 7 g | Fiber: 2 g | Sugar: 2 g**

# 33.Garlicky Sautéed Spinach with Lemon

★★☆☆☆

🕐 5 Minutes    ♨🕐 10 Minutes    🍴 4 servings

## INGREDIENTS

- 2 tablespoons olive oil
- 3 cloves garlic, minced
- 1 pound fresh spinach, washed and dried
- Salt and pepper to taste
- 1 lemon, cut into wedges

## INSTRUCTIONS

1. Heat Oil: Heat olive oil in a large skillet over medium heat.
2. Sauté Garlic: Add minced garlic and sauté for 1-2 minutes until fragrant.
3. Cook Spinach: Add the spinach to the skillet in batches, cooking until wilted, about 3-5 minutes.
4. Season: Season with salt and pepper to taste.
5. Serve: Transfer the spinach to a serving dish, drizzle with lemon juice from the wedges, and serve hot.

**Nutritional :Calories: 80 kcal | Protein: 2 g | Carbohydrates: 4 g | Fat: 7 g | Fiber: 2 g | Sugar: 1 g**

# 34.Zucchini Noodles with Tomatoes and Basil

★★★★☆

🕐 15 Minutes    ♨🕐 10 Minutes    🍴 4 servings

## INGREDIENTS

- 2 medium zucchinis, spiralized into noodles
- 2 cups cherry tomatoes, halved
- 3 cloves garlic, minced
- 2 tablespoons olive oil
- 1/4 cup fresh basil leaves, chopped
- 1/4 cup grated Parmesan cheese (optional)
- Salt and pepper to taste

## INSTRUCTIONS

1. Prepare Zucchini Noodles: Spiralize the zucchinis to create noodles and set them aside.
2. Cook Garlic: In a large skillet, heat olive oil over medium heat. Add minced garlic and sauté for 1-2 minutes until fragrant.
3. Add Tomatoes: Add cherry tomatoes to the skillet and cook for about 5 minutes until they start to soften.
4. Combine Noodles and Tomatoes: Add the zucchini noodles to the skillet and toss gently to combine. Cook for an additional 3-4 minutes until the noodles are tender but still crisp.
5. Season and Serve: Season with salt and pepper to taste. Garnish with fresh basil and sprinkle with Parmesan cheese if desired. Serve immediately.

**Nutritional: Calories: 150 kcal | Protein: 4 g | Carbohydrates: 10 g | Fat: 10 g | Fiber: 3 g | Sugar: 6 g**

# 35.Vegan Stuffed Bell Peppers with Quinoa and Black Beans

★★★★★

🕐 15 Minutes   ♨🕐 40 Minutes   🍴 4 servings

## INGREDIENTS

- 4 large bell peppers (any color), tops cut off and seeds removed
- 1 cup quinoa, rinsed
- 2 cups vegetable broth
- 1 can (15 oz) black beans, rinsed and drained
- 1 cup corn kernels (fresh, canned, or frozen)
- 1 cup diced tomatoes
- 1 small onion, finely chopped
- 2 cloves garlic, minced
- 1 teaspoon ground cumin
- 1 teaspoon chili powder
- Salt and pepper to taste
- 1/4 cup fresh cilantro, chopped
- 2 tablespoons olive oil

## INSTRUCTIONS

1. Preheat Oven: Preheat your oven to 375°F (190°C).
2. Cook Quinoa: In a medium saucepan, bring the vegetable broth to a boil. Add quinoa, reduce heat to low, cover, and simmer for about 15 minutes or until the quinoa is cooked and the broth is absorbed.
3. Prepare Filling: In a large skillet, heat olive oil over medium heat. Add onion and garlic, and sauté until the onion is translucent.
4. Combine Ingredients: Add the cooked quinoa, black beans, corn, diced tomatoes, cumin, chili powder, salt, and pepper to the skillet. Stir to combine and cook for an additional 5 minutes. Remove from heat and stir in the chopped cilantro.
5. Stuff Peppers: Place the bell peppers in a baking dish. Fill each pepper with the quinoa mixture, pressing down gently to pack the filling.
6. Bake: Cover the baking dish with aluminum foil and bake in the preheated oven for 30 minutes. Remove the foil and bake for an additional 10 minutes until the peppers are tender.
7. Serve: Serve the stuffed peppers hot, garnished with additional cilantro if desired.

**Nutritional: Calories: 250 kcal | Protein: 8 g | Carbohydrates: 45 g | Fat: 7 g | Fiber: 10 g | Sugar: 6 g**

# 36.Steamed Broccoli with Herbed Greek Yogurt Sauce

★★★★★

🕐 10 Minutes   ♨🕐 10 Minutes   🍴 4 servings

## INGREDIENTS

- 4 cups broccoli florets
- 1 cup Greek yogurt
- 2 tablespoons fresh parsley, chopped
- 1 tablespoon fresh dill, chopped
- 1 clove garlic, minced
- 1 tablespoon lemon juice
- Salt and pepper to taste

## INSTRUCTIONS

1. Steam Broccoli: In a large pot with a steamer basket, bring 1 inch of water to a boil. Add the broccoli florets, cover, and steam for about 5-7 minutes until tender but still crisp.
2. Prepare Sauce: In a small bowl, combine Greek yogurt, parsley, dill, garlic, lemon juice, salt, and pepper. Mix well.
3. Serve: Arrange the steamed broccoli on a serving plate and drizzle the herbed Greek yogurt sauce over the top.
4. Garnish: Garnish with additional fresh herbs if desired and serve immediately.

**Nutritional: Calories: 100 kcal | Protein: 6 g | Carbohydrates: 10 g | Fat: 4 g | Fiber: 4 g | Sugar: 3 g**

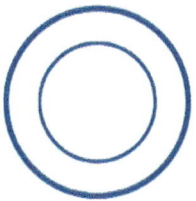 SEAFOOD

## 37. Grilled Salmon Fillet with Lemon and Dill Garnish

★★★★★

🕐 **5 Minutes**  ♨🕐 **10 Minutes**  🍴 **4 servings**

### INGREDIENTS

- 4 salmon fillets (6 ounces each)
- 2 tablespoons olive oil
- Salt and pepper to taste
- 1 lemon, sliced
- Fresh dill, for garnish

### INSTRUCTIONS

1. Preheat grill to medium-high heat.
2. Brush salmon fillets with olive oil and season with salt and pepper.
3. Grill salmon, skin side down, for 5 minutes. Flip carefully and place lemon slices on top. Grill for another 5 minutes or until cooked through.
4. Remove from grill and garnish with fresh dill.
5. Serve immediately.

**Nutritional: Calories: 280 kcal | Protein: 23 g | Carbohydrates: 0 g | Fat: 20 g | Fiber: 0 g | Sugar: 0 g**

## 38. Salmon Salad with Seafood Sauce

★★★★★

🕐 **15 Minutes**  ♨🕐 **0 Minutes**  🍴 **2 servings**

### INGREDIENTS

- 200g fresh salmon, thinly sliced
- 1 cup lettuce leaves
- 1 clove garlic, thinly sliced
- 1 small red chili, thinly sliced
- 2 tbsp seafood sauce (nam jim seafood)
- Fresh mint leaves for garnish

### INSTRUCTIONS

1. Prepare the Lettuce: Arrange the lettuce leaves on a serving plate as the base.
2. Add Salmon: Place the thinly sliced salmon over the lettuce.
3. Garnish: Top the salmon with thinly sliced garlic and red chili.
4. Drizzle with Sauce: Spoon the seafood sauce evenly over the salmon.
5. Garnish with Mint: Add fresh mint leaves on top for garnish.
6. Serve: Serve immediately and enjoy this fresh, flavorful salad.

**Nutrition: Calories: 180 kcal | Protein: 20 g | Carbs: 2 g | Fat: 10 g | Fiber: 0 g | Sugar: 1 g**

# 39.Spicy Garlic Shrimp

★★☆☆☆

5 Minutes   10 Minutes   4 servings

## INGREDIENTS

- 1 pound large shrimp, peeled and deveined
- 2 tablespoons olive oil
- 4 cloves garlic, minced
- 1 teaspoon red pepper flakes
- 1 tablespoon fresh lemon juice
- 2 tablespoons chopped fresh parsley
- Salt and pepper to taste

## INSTRUCTIONS

1. Heat olive oil in a large skillet over medium-high heat.
2. Add minced garlic and red pepper flakes to the skillet. Sauté for about 1 minute until fragrant.
3. Add the shrimp to the skillet. Cook for 2-3 minutes on each side until the shrimp turn pink and opaque.
4. Squeeze fresh lemon juice over the shrimp and stir to combine.
5. Season with salt and pepper to taste.
6. Garnish with chopped parsley before serving.
7. Serve immediately with a dipping sauce of your choice.

**Nutritional: Calories: 180 kcal, Protein: 24 g, Carbohydrates: 1 g, Fat: 8 g, Fiber: 0 g, Sugar: 0 g**

# 40.Seared Tuna Salad with Fresh Vegetables

★★☆☆☆

15 Minutes   0 Minutes   2 servings

## INGREDIENTS

- 2 tuna steaks (about 6 oz each)
- 2 tablespoons olive oil
- Salt and pepper to taste
- 1 cup cherry tomatoes, halved
- 1 cucumber, sliced
- 1 avocado, sliced
- 4 cups mixed salad greens
- 1/4 cup pine nuts, toasted
- Dressing:
- 2 tablespoons olive oil
- 1 tablespoon lemon juice
- 1 teaspoon Dijon mustard
- 1 teaspoon honey (optional)
- Salt and pepper to taste

## INSTRUCTIONS

1. Heat 2 tablespoons of olive oil in a skillet over medium-high heat.
2. Season tuna steaks with salt and pepper.
3. Sear tuna steaks for 2-3 minutes on each side, or until desired doneness. Remove from skillet and let rest for a few minutes.
4. In a large bowl, combine cherry tomatoes, cucumber, avocado, and mixed salad greens.
5. In a small bowl, whisk together the dressing ingredients: olive oil, lemon juice, Dijon mustard, honey (if using), salt, and pepper.
6. Slice the seared tuna steaks into thin slices.
7. Arrange the salad on plates, top with seared tuna slices, and sprinkle with toasted pine nuts.
8. Drizzle the dressing over the salad and serve immediately.

**Nutrition: Calories: 180 kcal | Protein: 20 g | Carbs: 2 g | Fat: 10 g | Fiber: 0 g | Sugar: 1 g**

# 41.Grilled Cod with Cherry Tomato Relish

★★★★☆

🕐 10 Minutes    🍳🕐 15 Minutes    🍴 4 servings

## INGREDIENTS

- 4 cod fillets (about 6 oz each)
- 2 tablespoons olive oil
- 1 teaspoon lemon zest
- Salt and pepper to taste
- 1 pint cherry tomatoes, halved
- 1 tablespoon fresh dill, chopped
- 1 tablespoon fresh parsley, chopped
- 1 tablespoon balsamic vinegar
- 2 cloves garlic, minced

## INSTRUCTIONS

1. Preheat the grill to medium-high heat.
2. Brush the cod fillets with olive oil and season with lemon zest, salt, and pepper.
3. Grill the cod fillets for about 4-5 minutes on each side or until the fish flakes easily with a fork.
4. While the cod is grilling, prepare the cherry tomato relish. In a medium bowl, combine cherry tomatoes, dill, parsley, balsamic vinegar, and minced garlic. Mix well.
5. Once the cod is done, transfer it to a serving platter.
6. Spoon the cherry tomato relish over the grilled cod fillets.
7. Garnish with additional fresh herbs if desired.
8. Serve immediately.

**Nutritional: Calories: 260 kcal, Protein: 32 g, Carbohydrates: 6 g, Fat: 12 g, Fiber: 2 g, Sugar: 4 g**

# 42.Grilled Shrimp Skewers with Vegetables

★★★☆☆

🕐 15 Minutes    🍳🕐 0 Minutes    🍴 2 servings

## INGREDIENTS

- 1 pound large shrimp, peeled and deveined
- 1 red bell pepper, cut into 1-inch pieces
- 1 yellow bell pepper, cut into 1-inch pieces
- 1 zucchini, sliced into rounds
- 1 red onion, cut into wedges
- 2 tablespoons olive oil
- 2 cloves garlic, minced
- 1 teaspoon dried oregano
- 1 teaspoon dried thyme
- Salt and pepper to taste
- Fresh parsley, chopped for garnish
- Lemon wedges for serving

## INSTRUCTIONS

1. Preheat the grill to medium-high heat.
2. In a large bowl, combine olive oil, garlic, oregano, thyme, salt, and pepper. Add shrimp and vegetables, tossing to coat evenly.
3. Thread shrimp and vegetables onto skewers, alternating between shrimp and different vegetables.
4. Grill skewers for 3-4 minutes on each side, or until shrimp are opaque and vegetables are tender and slightly charred.
5. Remove skewers from the grill and transfer to a serving platter.
6. Garnish with chopped fresh parsley and serve with lemon wedges.

**Nutritional: Calories: 220 kcal, Protein: 23 g, Carbohydrates: 10 g, Fat: 10 g, Fiber: 3 g, Sugar: 4 g**

# 43.Herb-Crusted Cod with Asparagus

★★★★☆

⏱ 15 Minutes   🍳⏱ 20Minutes   🍴 4 servings

## INGREDIENTS

- 4 cod fillets (about 6 ounces each)
- 2 tablespoons olive oil
- 1 teaspoon fresh rosemary, chopped
- 1 teaspoon fresh thyme, chopped
- Salt and pepper to taste
- 1 pound asparagus, trimmed
- 1 lemon, sliced
- 1/2 cup plain Greek yogurt
- 1 tablespoon Dijon mustard
- 1 garlic clove, minced

## INSTRUCTIONS

1. Preheat the oven to 400°F (200°C).
2. In a small bowl, mix olive oil, rosemary, thyme, salt, and pepper. Brush the mixture onto the cod fillets.
3. Place cod fillets on a baking sheet lined with parchment paper.
4. Arrange asparagus and lemon slices around the cod fillets. Drizzle with a little olive oil and season with salt and pepper.
5. Bake in the preheated oven for 15-20 minutes, or until the cod is opaque and flakes easily with a fork.
6. While the cod and asparagus are baking, prepare the sauce by mixing Greek yogurt, Dijon mustard, and minced garlic in a small bowl.
7. Serve the herb-crusted cod with roasted asparagus, and drizzle the yogurt sauce on top. Garnish with additional rosemary and thyme if desired.

**Nutritional: Calories: 250 kcal, Protein: 30 g, Carbohydrates: 7 g, Fat: 10 g, Fiber: 3 g, Sugar: 2 g**

# 44.Roasted Tuna with Green Vegetables

★★★☆☆

⏱ 15 Minutes   🍳⏱ 15 Minutes   🍴 4 servings

## INSTRUCTIONS

1. Preheat the oven to 400°F (200°C).
2. In a small bowl, mix olive oil, Dijon mustard, lemon juice, salt, and pepper.
3. Brush the mixture onto the tuna steaks.
4. Place the tuna steaks on a baking sheet lined with parchment paper.
5. In a separate bowl, toss broccolini and baby bok choy with olive oil, garlic powder, onion powder, salt, and pepper.
6. Arrange the vegetables around the tuna steaks on the baking sheet.
7. Roast in the preheated oven for 10-15 minutes, or until the tuna is cooked to your desired doneness and the vegetables are tender.
8. Sprinkle sesame seeds and chopped green onions over the roasted vegetables and tuna before serving.
9. Serve hot with additional lemon wedges if desired.

## INGREDIENTS

- 4 tuna steaks (about 6 oz each)
- 2 tablespoons olive oil
- 1 teaspoon Dijon mustard
- 1 teaspoon lemon juice
- Salt and pepper to taste
- 1 pound broccolini, trimmed
- 1 bunch of baby bok choy, halved
- 1 teaspoon garlic powder
- 1 teaspoon onion powder
- 1 tablespoon sesame seeds
- 1/4 cup green onions, chopped

**Nutritional : Calories: 350 kcal, Protein: 36 g, Carbohydrates: 8 g, Fat: 18 g, Fiber: 4 g, Sugar: 3 g**

# 45.Grilled Tilapia with Citrus Vinaigrette

★★★☆☆

🕐 10 Minutes     ♨🕐 15 Minutes     🍴 4 servings

## INSTRUCTIONS

1. Preheat the grill to medium-high heat.
2. Brush tilapia fillets with olive oil and season with salt, pepper, garlic powder, and dried thyme.
3. Grill the tilapia fillets for about 4-5 minutes on each side, until the fish is opaque and flakes easily with a fork.
4. While the fish is grilling, prepare the citrus vinaigrette. In a small bowl, whisk together lemon juice, orange juice, honey, and Dijon mustard. Slowly drizzle in the extra virgin olive oil while whisking continuously until the dressing is emulsified.
5. Once the fish is cooked, transfer to a serving platter and drizzle with the citrus vinaigrette.
6. Garnish with fresh rosemary if desired and serve immediately.

## INGREDIENTS

- 4 tilapia fillets
- 2 tablespoons olive oil
- Salt and pepper to taste
- 1 teaspoon garlic powder
- 1 teaspoon dried thyme
- 1/4 cup fresh lemon juice
- 2 tablespoons orange juice
- 1 tablespoon honey
- 1 tablespoon Dijon mustard
- 1/4 cup extra virgin olive oil
- Fresh rosemary for garnish (optional)

**Nutritional: Calories: 300 kcal, Protein: 25 g, Carbohydrates: 5 g, Fat: 20 g, Fiber: 0 g, Sugar: 3 g**

# 46.Grilled Swordfish with Lemon Herb Butter

★★☆☆☆

🕐 15 Minutes     ♨🕐 0 Minutes     🍴 2 servings

## INSTRUCTIONS

1. Preheat the grill to medium-high heat.
2. Brush swordfish steaks with olive oil and season with salt, pepper, garlic powder, and paprika.
3. Grill the swordfish steaks for about 5-7 minutes on each side, until the fish is opaque and flakes easily with a fork.
4. While the fish is grilling, prepare the lemon herb butter. In a small bowl, combine melted butter, lemon juice, and chopped parsley.
5. Once the fish is cooked, transfer to a serving platter and drizzle with the lemon herb butter.
6. Serve with lemon wedges and grilled cherry tomatoes, if desired.

## INGREDIENTS

- 4 swordfish steaks
- 2 tablespoons olive oil
- Salt and pepper to taste
- 1 teaspoon garlic powder
- 1 teaspoon paprika
- 1/4 cup unsalted butter, melted
- 2 tablespoons fresh lemon juice
- 1 tablespoon fresh parsley, chopped
- Lemon wedges for serving
- Grilled cherry tomatoes for garnish (optional)

**Nutritional: Calories: 400 kcal, Protein: 34 g, Carbohydrates: 2 g, Fat: 28 g, Fiber: 0 g, Sugar: 1 g**

# 47. Grilled Tilapia with Asparagus and Pesto

★★★☆☆

🕐 15 Minutes    🍳🕐 15 Minutes    🍴 4 servings

## INGREDIENTS

- 4 tilapia fillets (about 6 ounces each)
- 2 tablespoons olive oil
- Salt and pepper to taste
- 1 pound asparagus, trimmed
- 1/2 cup fresh basil pesto (store-bought or homemade)
- 1/2 cup cherry tomatoes, diced
- 1 lemon, cut into wedges

## INSTRUCTIONS

1. Preheat the grill to medium-high heat.
2. Brush tilapia fillets with olive oil and season with salt and pepper.
3. Grill tilapia for about 4-5 minutes on each side, or until it flakes easily with a fork.
4. While the tilapia is grilling, toss the asparagus with a little olive oil, salt, and pepper.
5. Grill the asparagus for about 5-7 minutes, turning occasionally, until tender and slightly charred.
6. Once the tilapia and asparagus are done, plate the asparagus and top each serving with a tilapia fillet.
7. Spoon pesto over the top of each fillet and garnish with diced cherry tomatoes.
8. Serve with lemon wedges on the side.

**Nutritional : Calories: 320 kcal, Protein: 30 g, Carbohydrates: 8 g, Fat: 20 g, Fiber: 4 g, Sugar: 2 g**

# 48. Pan-Seared Salmon with Garlic Sautéed Kale

★★★☆☆

🕐 10 Minutes    🍳🕐 20 Minutes    🍴 4 servings

## INGREDIENTS

- 4 salmon fillets
- 2 tablespoons olive oil, divided
- 2 cloves garlic, minced
- Salt and pepper to taste
- 1 bunch kale, chopped
- 1/4 cup vegetable broth or water
- 1 tablespoon fresh lemon juice
- 1 teaspoon lemon zest
- Optional: chopped fresh parsley for garnish

## INSTRUCTIONS

1. Heat 1 tablespoon of olive oil in a large skillet over medium-high heat. Season the salmon fillets with salt and pepper.
2. Place the salmon fillets in the skillet, skin-side down, and cook for about 4-5 minutes until the skin is crispy. Flip the fillets and cook for another 3-4 minutes until the salmon is opaque and flakes easily with a fork. Remove from the skillet and set aside.
3. In the same skillet, heat the remaining 1 tablespoon of olive oil over medium heat. Add the minced garlic and sauté for about 1 minute until fragrant.
4. Add the chopped kale to the skillet, and season with salt and pepper. Sauté for 3-4 minutes until the kale begins to wilt.
5. Pour in the vegetable broth or water, cover the skillet, and let the kale steam for an additional 3-4 minutes until tender.
6. Stir in the lemon juice and lemon zest, and cook for another minute. Remove from heat.
7. Serve the salmon fillets on a bed of garlic sautéed kale, garnished with chopped fresh parsley if desired.

**Nutritional : Calories: 380 kcal, Protein: 35 g, Carbohydrates: 6 g, Fat: 24 g, Fiber: 2 g, Sugar: 1 g**

# 49.Grilled Scallops with Lemon Butter Sauce

★★★☆☆

🕐 **10 Minutes**  🍳🕐 **15 Minutes**  🍴 **4 servings**

## INSTRUCTIONS

1. Preheat your grill to medium-high heat.
2. Pat the scallops dry with a paper towel and season with salt and pepper.
3. Drizzle olive oil over the scallops and toss to coat.
4. Grill the scallops for about 2-3 minutes per side, until they are opaque and slightly charred.
5. While the scallops are grilling, melt the butter in a small saucepan over medium heat.
6. Add the minced garlic to the butter and sauté for about 1 minute until fragrant.
7. Stir in the lemon juice and zest, and cook for another 1-2 minutes until heated through.
8. Remove the scallops from the grill and place them on a serving plate.
9. Pour the lemon butter sauce over the scallops and garnish with chopped parsley.
10. Serve with lemon wedges on the side.

## INGREDIENTS

- 1 pound large sea scallops
- 2 tablespoons olive oil
- Salt and pepper to taste
- 2 tablespoons unsalted butter
- 1 clove garlic, minced
- 1/4 cup fresh lemon juice
- 1 teaspoon lemon zest
- 1 tablespoon chopped fresh parsley
- Lemon wedges for serving

**Nutritional : Calories: 380 kcal | Protein: 35 g | Carbohydrates: 6 g | Fat: 24 g | Fiber: 2 g | Sugar: 1 g**

# 50.Octopus Salad with Tomatoes and Parsley

★★★☆☆

🕐 **20 Minutes**  🍳🕐 **60 Minutes**  🍴 **4 servings**

## INSTRUCTIONS

1. Place the octopus in a large pot with lemon halves and bay leaves. Cover with water and bring to a boil. Reduce heat and simmer gently for about 1.5 hours or until the octopus is tender.
2. Remove the octopus from the water and let it cool. Once cooled, cut into bite-sized pieces.
3. In a large bowl, combine the octopus, cherry tomatoes, and parsley.
4. Whisk together olive oil, red wine vinegar, salt, and pepper in a small bowl. Pour over the octopus salad and toss to combine.
5. Refrigerate for at least one hour to allow flavors to meld.
6. Serve chilled, garnished with additional parsley if desired.

## INGREDIENTS

- 1 medium octopus, cleaned (about 2 pounds)
- 1 lemon, halved
- 2 bay leaves
- 1 cup cherry tomatoes, halved
- 1/4 cup chopped fresh parsley
- 1/4 cup olive oil
- 2 tablespoons red wine vinegar
- Salt and pepper to taste

**Nutritional : Calories: 270 kcal | Protein: 25 g | Carbohydrates: 6 g | Fat: 16 g | Fiber: 2 g | Sugar: 2 g**

# 51. Grilled Shrimp Tacos with Avocado Salsa

★★★☆☆

🕐 15 Minutes    🍳🕐 10 Minutes    🍴 4 servings

## INGREDIENTS

- 1 pound large shrimp, peeled and deveined
- 2 tablespoons olive oil
- 2 cloves garlic, minced
- 1 teaspoon chili powder
- Salt and pepper to taste
- 8 small corn tortillas
- 1 avocado, diced
- 1 cup cherry tomatoes, diced
- 1/4 cup red onion, finely chopped
- 1/4 cup fresh cilantro, chopped
- 2 tablespoons lime juice
- Lime wedges for serving

## INSTRUCTIONS

1. In a bowl, combine shrimp, olive oil, garlic, chili powder, salt, and pepper. Toss to coat.
2. Preheat a grill or grill pan to medium-high heat.
3. Grill the shrimp for about 2-3 minutes per side, until they are opaque and slightly charred.
4. While the shrimp are grilling, warm the tortillas on the grill for about 1 minute per side.
5. In a separate bowl, combine avocado, cherry tomatoes, red onion, cilantro, lime juice, salt, and pepper to make the salsa.
6. To assemble, place a few grilled shrimp on each tortilla, and top with avocado salsa.
7. Serve with lime wedges on the side.

**Nutritional : Calories: 320 kcal | Protein: 28 g | Carbohydrates: 25 g | Fat: 15 g | Fiber: 6 g | Sugar: 3 g**

# 52. Salmon Ceviche with Avocado

★★☆☆☆

🕐 15 Minutes    🍳🕐 0 Minutes    🍴 4 servings

## INGREDIENTS

- 1 pound fresh salmon, diced
- 2 avocados, diced
- 1/2 cup red onion, finely chopped
- 1/2 cup fresh cilantro, chopped
- 1/2 cup lime juice (about 4 limes)
- 1/2 cup grapefruit juice (optional for extra flavor)
- 1 jalapeno, finely chopped (optional)
- Salt and pepper to taste

## INSTRUCTIONS

1. In a large bowl, combine diced salmon, red onion, cilantro, lime juice, and grapefruit juice.
2. Mix well, ensuring the salmon is well-coated with the juices. Let it marinate in the refrigerator for at least 15 minutes.
3. Before serving, gently fold in the diced avocado and jalapeno (if using).
4. Season with salt and pepper to taste.
5. Serve chilled, garnished with additional cilantro if desired.

**Nutritional : Calories: 320 kcal | Protein: 25 g | Carbohydrates: 10 g | Fat: 22 g | Fiber: 7 g | Sugar: 2 g**

# 53.Salmon Sashimi with Cucumber and Dill

★★☆☆☆

🕐 10 Minutes   🍳🕐 0 Minutes   🍴 2 servings

## INGREDIENTS

- 200g fresh salmon, thinly sliced
- 1/2 cucumber, thinly sliced
- Fresh dill, for garnish
- Cherry tomatoes, halved
- Lemon wedges
- Salt and pepper to taste

## INSTRUCTIONS

1. Arrange the salmon slices neatly on a plate.
2. Place the cucumber slices and cherry tomatoes around the salmon.
3. Garnish with fresh dill.
4. Season with salt and pepper to taste.
5. Serve with lemon wedges on the side.

**Nutritional : Calories: 180 kcal | Protein: 18 g | Carbohydrates: 4 g | Fat: 11 g | Fiber: 1 g | Sugar: 2 g**

# 54.Steamed Snapper with Ginger and Soy Sauce

★★★☆☆

🕐 10 Minutes   🍳🕐 15Minutes   🍴 2 servings

## INGREDIENTS

- 2 snapper fillets
- 2 tablespoons soy sauce
- 1 tablespoon sesame oil
- 1 tablespoon rice vinegar
- 1 tablespoon grated ginger
- 1 clove garlic, minced
- 1 red bell pepper, julienned
- 2 green onions, julienned
- Fresh cilantro, for garnish

## INSTRUCTIONS

1. In a small bowl, mix soy sauce, sesame oil, rice vinegar, ginger, and garlic.
2. Place snapper fillets in a steamer and pour the soy sauce mixture over them.
3. Steam the snapper for 10-12 minutes, or until the fish is fully cooked and flaky.
4. Remove the snapper from the steamer and place on a serving plate.
5. Top with julienned red bell pepper and green onions.
6. Garnish with fresh cilantro before serving.

**Nutritional: Calories: 250 kcal | Protein: 35 g | Carbohydrates: 4 g | Fat: 10 g | Fiber: 1 g | Sugar: 2 g**

## 55. Shrimp Salad with Fresh Vegetables

★★★☆☆

🕐 15 Minutes    ♨🕐 10 Minutes    🍴 4 servings

### INGREDIENTS

- 1 pound large shrimp, peeled and deveined
- 2 tablespoons olive oil
- 1 teaspoon paprika
- 1 teaspoon garlic powder
- Salt and pepper to taste
- 4 cups mixed salad greens
- 1 cucumber, diced
- 1 cup cherry tomatoes, halved
- 1/2 red onion, thinly sliced
- 1 avocado, diced
- Fresh cilantro, chopped
- Dressing:
- 3 tablespoons olive oil
- 1 tablespoon lemon juice
- 1 teaspoon Dijon mustard
- Salt and pepper to taste

### INSTRUCTIONS

1. Instructions:
2. Preheat a grill or grill pan over medium-high heat.
3. Toss the shrimp with olive oil, paprika, garlic powder, salt, and pepper.
4. Grill the shrimp for 2-3 minutes on each side, until pink and opaque.
5. In a large bowl, combine the salad greens, cucumber, cherry tomatoes, red onion, and avocado.
6. In a small bowl, whisk together the dressing ingredients.
7. Add the grilled shrimp to the salad and toss with the dressing.
8. Garnish with fresh cilantro and serve immediately.

**Nutritional : Calories: 320 kcal | Protein: 28 g | Carbohydrates: 12 g | Fat: 18 g | Fiber: 4 g | Sugar: 3 g**

## 56. Sesame Crusted Ahi Tuna Salad

★★★☆☆

🕐 15 Minutes    ♨🕐 5 Minutes    🍴 2 servings

### INGREDIENTS

- 2 ahi tuna steaks
- 2 tablespoons soy sauce
- 1 tablespoon sesame oil
- 2 tablespoons black and white sesame seeds
- Salt and pepper to taste
- 4 cups mixed salad greens
- 1 cup cherry tomatoes, halved
- 1 cucumber, sliced
- 1 carrot, julienned
- 1 avocado, sliced
- Dressing:
- 2 tablespoons rice vinegar
- 1 tablespoon soy sauce
- 1 tablespoon sesame oil
- 1 teaspoon honey
- 1 teaspoon grated ginger

### INSTRUCTIONS

1. Marinate the tuna steaks in soy sauce and sesame oil for 10 minutes.
2. Mix the sesame seeds, salt, and pepper on a plate. Coat the tuna steaks with the sesame seed mixture.
3. Heat a non-stick skillet over medium-high heat and sear the tuna steaks for 1-2 minutes on each side.
4. Remove from heat and let rest for a few minutes before slicing thinly.
5. Arrange the salad greens, cherry tomatoes, cucumber, carrot, and avocado on a plate.
6. Top with sliced ahi tuna.
7. Whisk together the dressing ingredients and drizzle over the salad.

**Nutritional : Calories: 350 kcal | Protein: 30 g | Carbohydrates: 12 g | Fat: 20 g | Fiber: 5 g | Sugar: 4 g**

# 57.Shrimp Scampi Linguine with Cherry Tomatoes and Parsley

★★★★☆

🕐 10 Minutes    🍳🕐 10 Minutes    🍴 4 servings

## INGREDIENTS

- 12 oz linguine
- 2 tablespoons olive oil
- 1 pound shrimp, peeled and deveined
- 4 cloves garlic, minced
- 1/2 cup white wine
- 1 cup cherry tomatoes, halved
- Salt and pepper to taste
- 1/4 cup fresh parsley, chopped

## INSTRUCTIONS

1. Cook linguine according to package instructions until al dente. Drain and set aside.
2. In a large skillet, heat olive oil over medium heat. Add garlic and sauté for 1 minute.
3. Add shrimp and cook until pink and opaque, about 2-3 minutes per side.
4. Pour in white wine and add cherry tomatoes. Simmer for 2 minutes.
5. Toss cooked linguine with shrimp mixture. Season with salt and pepper.
6. Garnish with chopped parsley and serve immediately.

**Nutritional: Calories: 450 kcal | Protein: 28 g | Carbohydrates: 56 g | Fat: 12 g | Fiber: 3 g | Sugar: 4 g**

# 58.Grilled Shrimp and Pineapple Skewers with Sweet Chili Glaze

★★★☆☆

🕐 15 Minutes    🍳🕐 10 Minutes    🍴 4 servings

## INGREDIENTS

- 1 pound large shrimp, peeled and deveined
- 1 cup pineapple, cut into chunks
- 1/4 cup sweet chili sauce
- 1 tablespoon soy sauce
- 1 teaspoon garlic, minced
- 1 teaspoon ginger, minced
- 2 tablespoons lime juice
- Fresh cilantro, for garnish

## INSTRUCTIONS

1. Preheat grill to medium-high heat.
2. In a small bowl, mix sweet chili sauce, soy sauce, garlic, ginger, and lime juice.
3. Thread shrimp and pineapple chunks alternately onto skewers.
4. Brush the skewers with the chili sauce mixture.
5. Grill for 2-3 minutes per side or until shrimp are pink and cooked through.
6. Garnish with fresh cilantro before serving.

**Nutritional : Calories: 210 kcal | Protein: 24 g | Carbohydrates: 18 g | Fat: 4 g | Fiber: 1 g | Sugar: 15 g**

## 59.Stir-Fried Mixed Vegetables with Shrimp

★★★★☆

🕐 10 Minutes  ♨🕐 10 Minutes  🍴 4 servings

### INGREDIENTS

- 1 pound shrimp, peeled and deveined
- 2 tablespoons vegetable oil
- 1 red bell pepper, sliced
- 1 green bell pepper, sliced
- 1 onion, sliced
- 2 cloves garlic, minced
- 2 tablespoons soy sauce
- 1 tablespoon oyster sauce
- 1 teaspoon sesame oil
- Salt and pepper to taste

### INSTRUCTIONS

1. Heat vegetable oil in a large skillet or wok over medium-high heat.
2. Add garlic and onion, sauté for 2 minutes until fragrant.
3. Add red and green bell peppers, cook for an additional 3 minutes.
4. Add shrimp and stir-fry until they turn pink and are cooked through, about 3-4 minutes.
5. Stir in soy sauce, oyster sauce, and sesame oil. Mix well.
6. Season with salt and pepper.
7. Serve hot, ideally over a bed of steamed rice.

**Nutritional: Calories: 240 kcal | Protein: 24 g | Carbohydrates: 9 g | Fat: 12 g | Fiber: 2 g | Sugar: 4 g**

## 60. Grilled Striped Bass with Lemon and Herb

★★★☆☆

🕐 15 Minutes  ♨🕐 10 Minutes  🍴 4 servings

### INGREDIENTS

- 4 striped bass fillets (6 ounces each)
- 2 tablespoons olive oil
- 1 lemon, sliced
- 2 tablespoons fresh herbs (such as parsley, thyme, or dill), chopped
- Salt and pepper to taste

### INSTRUCTIONS

1. Preheat grill to medium-high heat.
2. Brush both sides of the bass fillets with olive oil. Season with salt and pepper.
3. Place lemon slices and a sprinkle of fresh herbs on each fillet.
4. Grill the fish, skin side down, without flipping, for about 10 minutes, or until the fish is opaque and flakes easily with a fork.
5. Serve hot, garnished with additional fresh herbs.

**Nutritional: Calories: 230 kcal | Protein: 23 g | Carbohydrates: 2 g | Fat: 14 g | Fiber: 0.5 g | Sugar: 0.5 g**

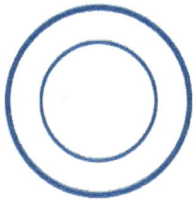 # MEAT

## 61.Grilled Lemon Herb Chicken Breast

★★★★☆

🕐 10 Minutes    🍳🕐 10 Minutes    🍴 4 servings

### INGREDIENTS

- 4 boneless, skinless chicken breasts
- 2 tablespoons olive oil
- 2 tablespoons lemon juice
- 2 garlic cloves, minced
- 1 teaspoon dried oregano
- 1 teaspoon dried thyme
- Salt and pepper to taste
- Fresh parsley for garnish

### INSTRUCTIONS

1. Preheat the grill to medium-high heat.
2. In a small bowl, mix together olive oil, lemon juice, garlic, oregano, thyme, salt, and pepper.
3. Brush the chicken breasts with the mixture, ensuring they are well coated.
4. Place the chicken on the grill and cook for 6-7 minutes on each side or until the internal temperature reaches 165°F (75°C).
5. Remove the chicken from the grill and let it rest for 5 minutes before serving.
6. Garnish with fresh parsley and serve with a side of your favorite green salad.

**Nutritional : Calories: 200 kcal | Protein: 30 g | Carbohydrates: 2 g | Fat: 7 g | Fiber: 0 g | Sugar: 0 g**

## 62.Grilled Balsamic Glazed Pork Chops

★★★☆☆

🕐 15 Minutes    🍳🕐 10 Minutes    🍴 4 servings

### INSTRUCTIONS

1. In a small bowl, whisk together balsamic vinegar, olive oil, soy sauce, honey, garlic, rosemary, salt, and pepper.
2. Place the pork chops in a resealable plastic bag or a shallow dish and pour the marinade over them. Seal the bag or cover the dish and refrigerate for at least 30 minutes, preferably overnight.
3. Preheat the grill to medium-high heat.
4. Remove the pork chops from the marinade and let any excess drip off.
5. Grill the pork chops for about 6-7 minutes per side or until the internal temperature reaches 145°F (63°C).
6. Let the pork chops rest for 5 minutes before serving.
7. Garnish with fresh chives and lemon wedges. Serve with your favorite steamed vegetables.

### INGREDIENTS

- 4 boneless pork chops
- 1/4 cup balsamic vinegar
- 2 tablespoons olive oil
- 2 tablespoons soy sauce (low sodium)
- 2 tablespoons honey
- 2 garlic cloves, minced
- 1 teaspoon dried rosemary
- Salt and pepper to taste
- Lemon wedges for garnish
- Fresh chives for garnish

**Nutritional : Calories: 380 kcal | Protein: 35 g | Carbohydrates: 6 g | Fat: 24 g | Fiber: 2 g | Sugar: 1 g**

# 63.Herb-Infused Chicken Meatballs

★★★★☆

🕐 15 Minutes    ♨🕐 20 Minutes    🍴 4 servings

## INGREDIENTS

- 500g ground chicken
- 1/2 cup breadcrumbs
- 1/4 cup grated Parmesan cheese
- 1/4 cup chopped fresh parsley
- 2 garlic cloves, minced
- 1 egg
- 1 tbsp olive oil
- 1 tsp dried oregano
- 1 tsp dried basil
- Salt and pepper to taste

## INSTRUCTIONS

1. Preheat the oven to 200°C (400°F) and line a baking sheet with parchment paper.
2. In a large bowl, combine the ground chicken, breadcrumbs, Parmesan cheese, parsley, garlic, egg, olive oil, oregano, basil, salt, and pepper. Mix until well combined.
3. Form the mixture into meatballs, about the size of a golf ball, and place them on the prepared baking sheet.
4. Bake in the preheated oven for 15-20 minutes or until the meatballs are golden brown and cooked through.
5. Serve warm with a side of your choice, such as a fresh green salad or steamed vegetables.

**Nutritional : Calories: 210 kcal | Protein: 22g | Carbohydrates: 6g | Fat: 11g | Fiber: 1g | Sugar: 1g**

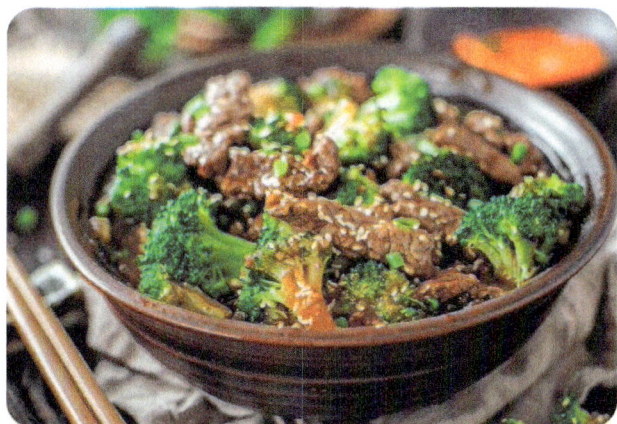

# 64.Beef and Broccoli Stir-Fry

★★★☆☆

🕐 10 Minutes    ♨🕐 15 Minutes    🍴 4 servings

## INGREDIENTS

- 500g beef sirloin, thinly sliced
- 2 cups broccoli florets
- 1 bell pepper, sliced
- 3 garlic cloves, minced
- 2 tbsp soy sauce (low sodium)
- 1 tbsp oyster sauce
- 1 tbsp hoisin sauce
- 1 tsp sesame oil
- 1 tsp cornstarch
- 1/2 cup beef broth
- 2 tbsp sesame seeds
- 2 green onions, chopped
- Salt and pepper to taste

## INSTRUCTIONS

1. In a small bowl, mix the soy sauce, oyster sauce, hoisin sauce, sesame oil, cornstarch, and beef broth. Set aside.
2. Heat a large wok or skillet over medium-high heat. Add a little oil, then stir-fry the beef slices until they are just cooked through. Remove and set aside.
3. In the same wok, add a little more oil if needed, then stir-fry the garlic until fragrant. Add the broccoli and bell pepper, and cook for about 5 minutes until they are tender-crisp.
4. Return the beef to the wok, then pour the sauce mixture over the beef and vegetables. Stir well to coat everything with the sauce. Cook for another 2-3 minutes until the sauce thickens.
5. Sprinkle with sesame seeds and chopped green onions before serving. Serve hot with a side of steamed rice or quinoa.

**Nutritional : Calories: 320 kcal | Protein: 30g | Carbohydrates: 12g | Fat: 18g | Fiber: 4g | Sugar: 5g**

# 65.Grilled Lamb Chops with Rosemary

★★★☆☆

🕐 10 Minutes    ♨🕐 15 Minutes    🍴 4 servings

## INGREDIENTS

- 8 lamb chops
- 2 tbsp olive oil
- 3 garlic cloves, minced
- 2 tbsp fresh rosemary, chopped
- Salt and pepper to taste
- Lemon wedges for serving

## INSTRUCTIONS

1. Preheat your grill to medium-high heat.
2. In a small bowl, mix the olive oil, minced garlic, chopped rosemary, salt, and pepper.
3. Brush the lamb chops with the olive oil mixture, ensuring they are evenly coated.
4. Grill the lamb chops for about 4-5 minutes on each side, or until they reach your desired level of doneness.
5. Remove from the grill and let rest for a few minutes before serving.
6. Serve with lemon wedges and garnish with additional rosemary if desired.

**Nutritional : Calories: 320 kcal | Protein: 24g | Carbohydrates: 0g | Fat: 25g | Fiber: 0g | Sugar: 0g**

# 66.Herb Fried Chicken

★★★☆☆

🕐 15 Minutes    ♨🕐 25 Minutes    🍴 4 servings

## INGREDIENTS

- 4 chicken thighs
- 2 tbsp olive oil
- 2 tsp garlic powder
- 1 tsp onion powder
- 2 tsp dried rosemary
- 1 tsp dried thyme
- Salt and pepper to taste

## INSTRUCTIONS

1. Preheat the oven to 200°C (400°F).
2. In a small bowl, mix the garlic powder, onion powder, dried rosemary, dried thyme, salt, and pepper.
3. Rub the chicken thighs with olive oil, then coat them with the herb mixture.
4. Heat a large oven-safe skillet over medium-high heat. Add the chicken thighs, skin side down, and cook for 3-4 minutes, until the skin is golden and crispy.
5. Flip the chicken thighs and transfer the skillet to the preheated oven.
6. Bake for 20-25 minutes, or until the chicken is cooked through and the internal temperature reaches 74°C (165°F).
7. Remove the chicken from the oven and let it rest for a few minutes before serving.

**Nutritional : Calories: 380 kcal | Protein: 28g | Carbohydrates: 2g | Fat: 28g | Fiber: 0g | Sugar: 0g**

## 67. Grilled Chicken Breast with Steamed Broccoli and Cherry Tomatoes

★★★☆☆

🕐 10 Minutes    ♨🕐 20Minutes    🍴 4 servings

### INGREDIENTS

- 4 boneless, skinless chicken breasts
- 2 tbsp olive oil
- 1 tsp garlic powder
- 1 tsp onion powder
- Salt and pepper to taste
- 2 cups broccoli florets
- 1 cup cherry tomatoes
- Fresh herbs for garnish (optional)

### INSTRUCTIONS

1. Preheat the grill to medium-high heat.
2. Rub the chicken breasts with olive oil, garlic powder, onion powder, salt, and pepper.
3. Grill the chicken for 6-8 minutes per side, or until the internal temperature reaches 74°C (165°F).
4. While the chicken is grilling, steam the broccoli until tender, about 5-7 minutes.
5. In the last few minutes of grilling, add the cherry tomatoes to the grill and cook until slightly charred.
6. Arrange the grilled chicken, steamed broccoli, and cherry tomatoes on a plate.
7. Garnish with fresh herbs if desired and serve warm.

**Nutritional: Calories: 280 kcal | Protein: 35g | Carbohydrates: 5g | Fat: 13g | Fiber: 3g | Sugar: 2g**

## 68. Paneer Tikka Skewers

★★★☆☆

🕐 15 Minutes    ♨🕐 20 Minutes    🍴 4 servings

### INGREDIENTS

- 200g paneer, cut into cubes
- 1 green bell pepper, cut into chunks
- 1 red onion, cut into chunks
- 2 tbsp plain yogurt
- 1 tbsp lemon juice
- 1 tbsp ginger-garlic paste
- 1 tsp cumin powder
- 1 tsp coriander powder
- 1/2 tsp turmeric powder
- 1 tsp paprika
- 1/2 tsp garam masala
- Salt to taste
- 1 tbsp olive oil
- Fresh cilantro for garnish

### INSTRUCTIONS

1. In a large bowl, mix yogurt, lemon juice, ginger-garlic paste, cumin powder, coriander powder, turmeric powder, paprika, garam masala, salt, and olive oil to create a marinade.
2. Add paneer cubes, bell pepper, and onion to the marinade. Toss to coat evenly. Let it marinate for at least 30 minutes.
3. Preheat the grill to medium-high heat.
4. Thread the marinated paneer, bell pepper, and onion onto skewers.
5. Grill the skewers for 10-15 minutes, turning occasionally, until the paneer is golden and the vegetables are tender.
6. Garnish with fresh cilantro and serve warm.

**Nutritional : Calories: 200 kcal | Protein: 12g | Carbohydrates: 8g | Fat: 14g | Fiber: 2g | Sugar: 4g**

# 69.Stuffed Bell Peppers

★★★★☆

🕐 20 Minutes      🍳🕐 40 Minutes      🍴 4 servings

## INGREDIENTS

- 4 large bell peppers (any color)
- 200g ground turkey or chicken
- 1 cup cooked quinoa
- 1 small onion, finely chopped
- 2 cloves garlic, minced
- 1 cup diced tomatoes (canned or fresh)
- 1/2 cup shredded mozzarella cheese
- 1 tbsp olive oil
- 1 tsp dried oregano
- 1 tsp dried basil
- Salt and pepper to taste
- Fresh parsley or dill for garnish

## INSTRUCTIONS

1. Preheat the oven to 180°C (350°F). Cut the tops off the bell peppers and remove the seeds and membranes.
2. In a large skillet, heat olive oil over medium heat. Add chopped onion and garlic, and sauté until softened, about 3-4 minutes.
3. Add ground turkey or chicken to the skillet. Cook until browned, breaking it up with a spoon as it cooks.
4. Stir in cooked quinoa, diced tomatoes, oregano, basil, salt, and pepper. Cook for another 2-3 minutes until well combined.
5. Stuff each bell pepper with the turkey-quinoa mixture. Place the stuffed peppers in a baking dish.
6. Sprinkle shredded mozzarella cheese on top of each stuffed pepper.
7. Cover the baking dish with foil and bake for 30 minutes. Remove the foil and bake for an additional 10 minutes until the cheese is melted and bubbly.
8. Garnish with fresh parsley or dill before serving.

**Nutritional: Calories: 280 kcal | Protein: 22g | Carbohydrates: 24g | Fat: 12g | Fiber: 5g | Sugar: 8g**

# 70.Malai Chicken with Yogurt Sauce

★★★★☆

🕐 20 Minutes      🍳🕐 30 Minutes      🍴 4 servings

## INGREDIENTS

- 500g chicken drumsticks
- 1 cup Greek yogurt
- 1/2 cup fresh cream
- 2 tbsp lemon juice
- 2 cloves garlic, minced
- 1 inch ginger, minced
- 1 green chili, finely chopped
- 1 tsp garam masala
- 1 tsp ground cumin
- 1 tsp ground coriander
- Salt and pepper to taste
- Fresh cilantro leaves for garnish

## INSTRUCTIONS

1. In a large bowl, mix Greek yogurt, fresh cream, lemon juice, minced garlic, minced ginger, chopped green chili, garam masala, ground cumin, ground coriander, salt, and pepper.
2. Add the chicken drumsticks to the marinade, making sure they are well-coated. Cover and refrigerate for at least 2 hours, preferably overnight.
3. Preheat the oven to 200°C (400°F). Line a baking sheet with parchment paper.
4. Arrange the marinated chicken drumsticks on the prepared baking sheet.
5. Bake in the preheated oven for 25-30 minutes, until the chicken is cooked through and slightly charred on the edges.
6. While the chicken is baking, prepare the yogurt sauce. In a small bowl, mix 1 cup of Greek yogurt with a pinch of salt, minced garlic, and chopped cilantro.
7. Serve the baked Malai chicken with the yogurt sauce, garnished with fresh cilantro leaves.

**Nutritional : Calories: 320 kcal | Protein: 30g | Carbohydrates: 6g | Fat: 18g | Fiber: 0.5g | Sugar: 4g**

# 71.Sweet and Spicy Chicken Wings

★★★☆☆

🕐 15 Minutes   ♨🕐 40 Minutes   🍴 4 servings

## INSTRUCTIONS

1. Preheat the oven to 200°C (400°F). Line a baking sheet with parchment paper.
2. In a large bowl, mix soy sauce, honey, chili sauce, olive oil, minced garlic, grated ginger, and ground black pepper to make the marinade.
3. Add the chicken wings to the bowl and toss to coat evenly with the marinade. Let it sit for 10 minutes.
4. Arrange the marinated chicken wings on the prepared baking sheet in a single layer.
5. Bake in the preheated oven for 35-40 minutes, turning the wings halfway through, until they are golden brown and fully cooked.
6. Remove from the oven and let them cool for a few minutes.
7. Transfer the wings to a serving bowl and garnish with fresh chopped parsley.

## INGREDIENTS

- 1 kg chicken wings
- 1/2 cup soy sauce
- 1/4 cup honey
- 1/4 cup chili sauce
- 2 tbsp olive oil
- 1 tbsp minced garlic
- 1 tbsp grated ginger
- 1 tsp ground black pepper
- Fresh parsley, chopped, for garnish

**Nutritional : Calories: 360 kcal | Protein: 28g | Carbohydrates: 12g | Fat: 22g | Fiber: 0.5g | Sugar: 9g**

# 72.Grilled Pork Chop with Peach Glaze

★★★☆☆

🕐 15 Minutes   ♨🕐 25 Minutes   🍴 4 servings

## INSTRUCTIONS

1. Preheat the grill to medium-high heat.
2. In a small bowl, combine peach preserves, apple cider vinegar, olive oil, minced garlic, and chopped rosemary. Mix well to create the glaze.
3. Season the pork chops with salt and pepper on both sides.
4. Grill the pork chops for about 4-5 minutes on each side, or until the internal temperature reaches 145°F (63°C).
5. While grilling, brush the peach glaze onto the pork chops during the last few minutes of cooking.
6. Grill the peach halves cut side down for 2-3 minutes until they are caramelized and have grill marks.
7. Remove the pork chops and peaches from the grill and let them rest for a few minutes.
8. Serve the pork chops with the grilled peach halves and garnish with fresh rosemary sprigs.

## INGREDIENTS

- 4 pork chops (about 1-inch thick)
- 2 peaches, halved and pitted
- 1/4 cup peach preserves
- 2 tbsp apple cider vinegar
- 1 tbsp olive oil
- 2 cloves garlic, minced
- 1 tbsp fresh rosemary, chopped
- Salt and pepper to taste
- Fresh rosemary sprigs for garnish

**Nutritional : Calories: 320 kcal | Protein: 30g | Carbohydrates: 6g | Fat: 18g | Fiber: 0.5g | Sugar: 4g**

# 73.Grilled Chicken Salad

★★★☆☆

🕐 15 Minutes   ♨🕐 20 Minutes   🍴 4 servings

## INGREDIENTS

- 2 boneless, skinless chicken breasts
- 1 tbsp olive oil
- Salt and pepper to taste
- 4 cups mixed salad greens
- 1 cup cherry tomatoes, halved
- 1 cucumber, sliced
- 1/4 red onion, thinly sliced
- 1/4 cup feta cheese, crumbled
- 1/4 cup balsamic vinaigrette

## INSTRUCTIONS

1. Prepare the Chicken: Preheat the grill to medium-high heat. Brush the chicken breasts with olive oil and season with salt and pepper. Grill the chicken for 6-7 minutes on each side, or until fully cooked. Let the chicken rest for 5 minutes before slicing.
2. Assemble the Salad: In a large bowl, combine the salad greens, cherry tomatoes, cucumber, and red onion. Top with the sliced grilled chicken.
3. Serve: Drizzle the balsamic vinaigrette over the salad. Sprinkle with feta cheese and serve immediately.

**Nutritional : Calories: 350 kcal | Protein: 30g | Carbohydrates: 10g | Fat: 20g | Fiber: 3g | Sugar: 5g**

# 74.Grilled Sausages with Mashed Potatoes and Onion Gravy

★★★☆☆

🕐 15 Minutes   ♨🕐 25 Minutes   🍴 4 servings

## INGREDIENTS

- 4 chicken sausages
- 1 tbsp olive oil
- 1 large onion, thinly sliced
- 2 cups chicken broth, low sodium
- 1 tbsp cornstarch
- 1/4 cup cold water
- 4 large potatoes, peeled and cubed
- 1/4 cup milk
- 2 tbsp butter
- Salt and pepper to taste
- Fresh parsley, chopped (for garnish)

## INSTRUCTIONS

1. Prepare the Mashed Potatoes: Boil the potatoes in salted water until tender, about 15 minutes. Drain and mash the potatoes with milk, butter, salt, and pepper until smooth. Set aside and keep warm.
2. Cook the Sausages: Preheat the grill to medium heat. Grill the sausages for about 8-10 minutes, turning occasionally until fully cooked.
3. Make the Onion Gravy: In a large skillet, heat olive oil over medium heat. Add the sliced onion and cook until caramelized, about 10 minutes. Add the chicken broth and bring to a boil. In a small bowl, mix cornstarch with cold water until smooth, then stir into the gravy. Cook, stirring constantly, until the gravy thickens. Season with salt and pepper to taste.
4. Assemble and Serve: Place a generous scoop of mashed potatoes on each plate. Top with grilled sausages and pour onion gravy over the sausages and potatoes. Garnish with chopped fresh parsley and serve immediately.

**Nutritional : Calories: 410 kcal | Protein: 18g | Carbohydrates: 45g | Fat: 18g | Fiber: 5g | Sugar: 6g**

# 75. Honey Mustard Glazed Chicken Thighs

★★★☆☆

🕐 10 Minutes    ♨🕐 30 Minutes    🍴 4 servings

## INGREDIENTS

- 8 chicken thighs, skin-on and bone-in
- 1/4 cup honey
- 1/4 cup Dijon mustard
- 2 tbsp soy sauce, low sodium
- 2 cloves garlic, minced
- 1 tbsp olive oil
- Salt and pepper to taste
- Fresh parsley, chopped (for garnish)

## INSTRUCTIONS

1. Preheat the Oven: Preheat your oven to 200°C (400°F).
2. Prepare the Glaze: In a small bowl, whisk together honey, Dijon mustard, soy sauce, minced garlic, and olive oil until well combined.
3. Season the Chicken: Pat the chicken thighs dry with paper towels and season both sides with salt and pepper.
4. Coat the Chicken: Place the chicken thighs in a large bowl or resealable plastic bag. Pour the honey mustard glaze over the chicken and toss to coat evenly.
5. Bake the Chicken: Arrange the chicken thighs on a baking sheet lined with parchment paper or aluminum foil, skin side up. Bake in the preheated oven for 25-30 minutes, or until the internal temperature of the chicken reaches 74°C (165°F) and the skin is golden and crispy.
6. Serve: Transfer the chicken thighs to a serving platter and garnish with chopped fresh parsley. Serve warm with your favorite sides.

**Nutritional: Calories: 350 kcal | Protein: 25g | Carbohydrates: 15g | Fat: 20g | Fiber: 0g | Sugar: 14g**

# 76. Stuffed Chicken Breast with Spinach and Mushrooms

★★★★☆

🕐 15 Minutes    ♨🕐 25 Minutes    🍴 4 servings

## INSTRUCTIONS

1. Preheat the Oven: Preheat your oven to 200°C (400°F).
2. Prepare the Filling: Heat 1 tbsp of olive oil in a skillet over medium heat. Add minced garlic and sliced mushrooms to the skillet and sauté until the mushrooms are soft. Add spinach to the skillet and cook until wilted. Season with salt, pepper, and oregano. Remove from heat and let cool slightly. Stir in the shredded mozzarella cheese.
3. Prepare the Chicken: Cut a horizontal slit along the thin side of each chicken breast to create a pocket, being careful not to cut all the way through. Stuff each chicken breast with the spinach and mushroom mixture, securing with toothpicks if necessary. Season the outside of the chicken breasts with salt and pepper.
4. Cook the Chicken: Heat the remaining 1 tbsp of olive oil in an oven-safe skillet over medium-high heat. Add the stuffed chicken breasts and cook for 3-4 minutes on each side, until golden brown. Transfer the skillet to the preheated oven and bake for 20-25 minutes, or until the chicken is cooked through and the internal temperature reaches 74°C (165°F).
5. Serve: Remove the toothpicks and transfer the stuffed chicken breasts to a serving plate. Serve warm with your favorite sides.

## INGREDIENTS

- 4 boneless, skinless chicken breasts
- 2 cups fresh spinach leaves
- 1 cup mushrooms, sliced
- 1/2 cup mozzarella cheese, shredded
- 2 cloves garlic, minced
- 2 tbsp olive oil
- 1 tsp dried oregano
- Salt and pepper to taste

**Nutritional: Calories: 320 kcal | Protein: 40g | Carbohydrates: 6g | Fat: 15g | Fiber: 2g | Sugar: 1g**

# 77.Chicken and Broccoli Stir-Fry

★★★★☆

🕐 10 Minutes   🍳🕐 15Minutes   🍴 4 servings

## INGREDIENTS

- 2 chicken breasts, cut into bite-sized pieces
- 4 cups broccoli florets
- 2 cloves garlic, minced
- 1 tbsp ginger, minced
- 2 tbsp soy sauce (low sodium)
- 1 tbsp oyster sauce
- 1 tbsp olive oil
- 1 tsp sesame oil
- 1/2 cup chicken broth (low sodium)
- 1 tbsp cornstarch mixed with 2 tbsp water (for thickening)
- Salt and pepper to taste
- Sesame seeds and chopped green onions for garnish (optional)

## INSTRUCTIONS

1. Prepare the Chicken: Season the chicken pieces with salt and pepper.
2. Cook the Chicken: Heat olive oil in a large skillet or wok over medium-high heat. Add the chicken and cook until it is browned and cooked through, about 5-7 minutes. Remove the chicken from the skillet and set aside.
3. Cook the Vegetables: In the same skillet, add garlic and ginger. Sauté for about 1 minute until fragrant. Add the broccoli florets and stir-fry for 3-4 minutes until they are bright green and tender-crisp.
4. Combine Ingredients: Return the chicken to the skillet with the broccoli. Add the soy sauce, oyster sauce, sesame oil, and chicken broth. Stir to combine.
5. Thicken the Sauce: Pour the cornstarch mixture into the skillet, stirring continuously until the sauce thickens, about 1-2 minutes.
6. Serve: Transfer the chicken and broccoli stir-fry to a serving bowl. Garnish with sesame seeds and chopped green onions if desired. Serve warm, ideally over a bed of brown rice or quinoa.

**Nutritional : Calories: 280 kcal | Protein: 30g | Carbohydrates: 10g | Fat: 12g | Fiber: 3g | Sugar: 2g**

# 78.Beef Bourguignon with Carrots and Onions

★★★☆☆

🕐 20 Minutes   🍳🕐 120 Minutes   🍴 4 servings

## INSTRUCTIONS

1. Prepare the Beef: Season the beef chunks with salt and pepper. Toss the beef in flour to lightly coat.
2. Sear the Beef: In a large pot or Dutch oven, heat olive oil over medium-high heat. Add the beef chunks and sear until browned on all sides. Remove from pot and set aside.
3. Cook the Vegetables: In the same pot, add the chopped onion and carrots. Sauté until the onion is translucent. Add minced garlic and cook for another minute.
4. Deglaze and Simmer: Pour in the red wine (or beef broth) to deglaze the pot, scraping up any browned bits from the bottom. Stir in tomato paste, beef broth, thyme, and the seared beef.
5. Simmer the Stew: Bring the mixture to a boil, then reduce heat to low. Cover and simmer for 1.5 to 2 hours, or until the beef is tender and the flavors have melded together.
6. Finish and Serve: Stir in chopped parsley. Adjust seasoning with salt and pepper if needed. Serve hot, garnished with additional parsley if desired.

## INGREDIENTS

- 1 lb (450g) beef stew meat, cut into chunks
- 2 cups carrots, sliced
- 1 large onion, chopped
- 2 cloves garlic, minced
- 1 cup red wine (optional, can use beef broth)
- 2 cups beef broth (low sodium)
- 2 tbsp tomato paste
- 1 tbsp olive oil
- 1 tbsp flour
- 2 tbsp fresh parsley, chopped
- 1 tsp dried thyme
- Salt and pepper to taste

**Nutritional : Calories: 320 kcal | Protein: 25g | Carbohydrates: 12g | Fat: 18g | Fiber: 3g | Sugar: 5g**

# 79.Grilled Chicken with Apple Slices

★★★☆☆

🕐 15 Minutes    🍳🕐 20 Minutes    🍴 4 servings

## INGREDIENTS

- 4 boneless, skinless chicken breasts
- 2 apples, cored and sliced
- 2 tbsp olive oil
- 1 tbsp balsamic vinegar
- 1 tbsp honey
- 1 tsp ground cinnamon
- Salt and pepper to taste
- Fresh parsley for garnish (optional)

## INSTRUCTIONS

1. Prepare the Chicken: Preheat your grill to medium-high heat. Season the chicken breasts with salt and pepper.
2. Marinate the Apples: In a bowl, combine olive oil, balsamic vinegar, honey, and ground cinnamon. Add apple slices to the mixture, ensuring they are well coated.
3. Grill the Chicken: Place the chicken breasts on the preheated grill. Grill for about 6-7 minutes per side, or until the internal temperature reaches 165°F (75°C) and the chicken is fully cooked.
4. Grill the Apples: During the last few minutes of grilling the chicken, place the marinated apple slices on the grill. Grill the apples for 2-3 minutes per side, or until they are tender and have grill marks.
5. Serve: Transfer the grilled chicken breasts to a serving plate. Arrange the grilled apple slices around the chicken. Drizzle any remaining balsamic-honey mixture over the chicken and apples. Garnish with fresh parsley if desired.

**Nutritional : Calories: 280 kcal | Protein: 30g | Carbohydrates: 10g | Fat: 12g | Fiber: 3g | Sugar: 2g**

# 80.Porchetta with Tangy Raspberry Coulis

★★★★☆

🕐 20 Minutes    🍳🕐 120 Minutes    🍴 4 servings

## INSTRUCTIONS

1. Prepare the Pork: Preheat your oven to 175°C (350°F). In a small bowl, mix olive oil, rosemary, thyme, minced garlic, salt, and pepper. Rub the mixture all over the pork loin.
2. Roast the Pork: Place the pork loin in a roasting pan. Roast in the preheated oven for about 2 hours or until the internal temperature reaches 145°F (63°C). Let the pork rest for 10 minutes before slicing.
3. Prepare the Raspberry Coulis: In a small saucepan, combine raspberries, honey, and balsamic vinegar. Cook over medium heat, stirring occasionally, until the raspberries break down and the sauce thickens (about 10 minutes). Strain the sauce through a fine mesh sieve to remove the seeds.
4. Serve: Slice the roasted pork loin and arrange it on a serving platter. Drizzle the raspberry coulis over the pork slices. Garnish with fresh raspberries and mint leaves.

## INGREDIENTS

- 1 boneless pork loin (about 2 pounds)
- 2 tbsp olive oil
- 1 tbsp fresh rosemary, chopped
- 1 tbsp fresh thyme, chopped
- 4 cloves garlic, minced
- Salt and pepper to taste
- 1 cup fresh raspberries
- 2 tbsp honey
- 1 tbsp balsamic vinegar
- Fresh mint leaves for garnish (optional)

**Nutritional : Calories: 350 kcal | Protein: 25g | Carbohydrates: 15g | Fat: 20g | Fiber: 2g | Sugar: 10g**

# 81.Grilled Steak with Roasted Vegetables

★★★☆☆

🕐 15 Minutes     🍳🕐 20 Minutes     🍴 4 servings

## INGREDIENTS

- 4 boneless steaks (about 6 oz each)
- 2 tbsp olive oil
- 1 tbsp fresh rosemary, chopped
- 1 tbsp fresh thyme, chopped
- 4 cloves garlic, minced
- Salt and pepper to taste
- 1 red bell pepper, sliced
- 1 yellow bell pepper, sliced
- 1 zucchini, sliced
- 1 lemon, halved
- Fresh rosemary and thyme sprigs for garnish

## INSTRUCTIONS

1. Prepare the Steaks: Preheat your grill to medium-high heat. In a small bowl, mix olive oil, chopped rosemary, thyme, minced garlic, salt, and pepper. Rub the mixture evenly over both sides of the steaks.
2. Grill the Steaks: Place the steaks on the preheated grill. Grill for about 4-5 minutes per side for medium-rare, or until the desired doneness is reached. Remove the steaks from the grill and let them rest for 5 minutes before slicing.
3. Roast the Vegetables: While the steaks are grilling, place the sliced bell peppers, zucchini, and lemon halves on the grill. Grill the vegetables for about 5-7 minutes, turning occasionally, until they are tender and have grill marks. Remove from the grill and set aside.
4. Serve: Slice the grilled steaks and arrange them on a serving platter. Add the grilled vegetables around the steak slices. Squeeze the grilled lemon juice over the steaks and vegetables. Garnish with fresh rosemary and thyme sprigs.

**Nutritional : Calories: 450 kcal | Protein: 35g | Carbohydrates: 8g | Fat: 30g | Fiber: 3g | Sugar: 4g**

# 82.Roasted Chicken Breast with Pumpkin and Spinach

★★★☆☆

🕐 15 Minutes     🍳🕐 30 Minutes     🍴 4 servings

## INGREDIENTS

- 4 boneless, skinless chicken breasts
- 2 cups diced pumpkin
- 2 tbsp olive oil
- 1 tsp garlic powder
- 1 tsp paprika
- Salt and pepper to taste
- 2 cups fresh spinach leaves

## INSTRUCTIONS

1. Preheat the Oven: Preheat your oven to 200°C (400°F).
2. Season the Chicken and Pumpkin: In a large bowl, mix olive oil, garlic powder, paprika, salt, and pepper. Toss the chicken breasts in the seasoning mixture until well coated. Place the diced pumpkin in the same bowl and toss to coat with the remaining seasoning.
3. Roast the Chicken and Pumpkin: Arrange the chicken breasts and diced pumpkin in a single layer on a baking sheet. Roast in the preheated oven for 25-30 minutes, or until the chicken is cooked through and the pumpkin is tender.
4. Serve: Arrange fresh spinach leaves on a serving plate. Place the roasted chicken breasts and pumpkin cubes on top of the spinach. Serve immediately.

**Nutritional : Calories: 320 kcal | Protein: 28g | Carbohydrates: 12g | Fat: 18g | Fiber: 4g | Sugar: 4g**

## 83.Meatballs with Tomato Sauce, Bell Pepper, Spring Onion, and Mint

★★★★☆

🕐 20 Minutes | 🍳🕐 30 Minutes | 🍴 4 servings

### INGREDIENTS

- 1 pound ground beef
- 1/4 cup breadcrumbs
- 1 egg
- 2 garlic cloves, minced
- 1/4 cup chopped fresh mint
- Salt and pepper to taste
- 1 tablespoon olive oil
- 1 bell pepper, diced
- 1/2 cup chopped spring onions
- 1 can (14 oz) crushed tomatoes
- 1 teaspoon sugar

### INSTRUCTIONS

1. In a bowl, mix ground beef, breadcrumbs, egg, garlic, mint, salt, and pepper until well combined.
2. Form into small meatballs, about 1 inch in diameter.
3. Heat olive oil in a skillet over medium heat. Add meatballs and brown on all sides.
4. Remove meatballs and set aside. In the same skillet, add bell pepper and spring onions. Cook until soft.
5. Add crushed tomatoes and sugar, bring to a simmer.
6. Return meatballs to the skillet, cover, and simmer for 20 minutes.
7. Serve hot, garnished with extra chopped mint.

**Nutritional : Calories: 380 kcal | Protein: 25 g | Carbohydrates: 15 g | Fat: 24 g | Fiber: 3 g | Sugar: 7 g**

## 84.Roasted Beef with Mashed Potatoes

★★★☆☆

🕐 20 Minutes | 🍳🕐 90 Minutes | 🍴 4 servings

### INSTRUCTIONS

1. Preheat oven to 350°F (175°C).
2. Rub the beef roast with olive oil, salt, and pepper.
3. Place in a roasting pan and roast in the preheated oven for about 1 hour 30 minutes, or until the internal temperature reaches 145°F (63°C) for medium rare.
4. Meanwhile, boil the potatoes in salted water until tender, about 20 minutes.
5. Drain potatoes and mash with milk, butter, and sour cream until smooth. Season with salt and pepper.
6. Slice the roasted beef and serve with the mashed potatoes. Garnish with chopped chives.

### INGREDIENTS

- 2 pounds beef roast
- 2 tablespoons olive oil
- Salt and pepper to taste
- 4 large potatoes, peeled and quartered
- 1/4 cup milk
- 2 tablespoons butter
- 1/4 cup sour cream
- Fresh chives, chopped for garnish

**Nutritional : Calories: 750 kcal | Protein: 45 g | Carbohydrates: 40 g | Fat: 45 g | Fiber: 3 g | Sugar: 3 g**

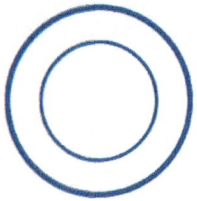

# VEGAN

## 85.Buckwheat Salad with Cherry Tomatoes and Red Onion

★★★☆☆

🕐 **10 Minutes**  🍳🕐 **20 Minutes**  🍴 **4 servings**

### INSTRUCTIONS

1. Cook the Buckwheat: Rinse the buckwheat groats under cold water. In a medium saucepan, bring the water to a boil. Add the buckwheat and a pinch of salt. Reduce the heat to low, cover, and simmer for about 15 minutes or until the buckwheat is tender and the water is absorbed. Let it cool.
2. Prepare the Salad: In a large bowl, combine the cooked buckwheat, cherry tomatoes, red onion, and chopped parsley.
3. Make the Dressing In a small bowl, whisk together the olive oil, lemon juice, salt, and pepper.
4. Toss and Serve: Pour the dressing over the salad and toss gently to combine. Adjust seasoning with salt and pepper if needed. Serve immediately or refrigerate for 30 minutes to let the flavors meld.

### INGREDIENTS

- 1 cup buckwheat groats
- 2 cups water
- 1 cup cherry tomatoes, halved
- 1/2 red onion, thinly sliced
- 1/4 cup fresh parsley, chopped
- 2 tbsp olive oil
- 1 tbsp lemon juice
- Salt and pepper to taste

**Nutritional : Calories: 190 kcal | Protein: 6g | Carbohydrates: 30g | Fat: 7g | Fiber: 5g | Sugar: 3g**

## 86.Zucchini Noodles with Cherry Tomatoes and Basil

★★★☆☆

🕐 **15 Minutes**  🍳🕐 **10 Minutes**  🍴 **4 servings**

### INSTRUCTIONS

1. Prepare the Zucchini Noodles: Spiralize the zucchinis using a spiralizer to create noodle-like strands. Set aside.
2. Cook the Garlic: In a large skillet, heat the olive oil over medium heat. Add the minced garlic and sauté for about 1 minute, or until fragrant.
3. Add the Zucchini Noodles: Add the spiralized zucchini to the skillet and cook for 2-3 minutes, tossing gently, until they are just tender but still firm.
4. Combine with Cherry Tomatoes: Add the halved cherry tomatoes to the skillet and toss with the zucchini noodles for another minute.
5. Season and Serve: Remove from heat. Season with salt and pepper to taste. Transfer to a serving bowl. Top with fresh basil leaves and grated Parmesan cheese. Serve immediately.

### INGREDIENTS

- 4 medium zucchinis, spiralized
- 1 cup cherry tomatoes, halved
- 1/4 cup fresh basil leaves
- 1/4 cup grated Parmesan cheese
- 2 tbsp olive oil
- 2 cloves garlic, minced
- Salt and pepper to taste

**Nutritional : Calories: 120 kcal | Protein: 4g | Carbohydrates: 8g | Fat: 8g | Fiber: 3g | Sugar: 5g**

# 87.Hearty Lentil Soup

★★★★★

🕐 **15 Minutes**  ♨🕐 **45 Minutes**  🍴 **6 servings**

## INGREDIENTS

- 1 cup dried lentils, rinsed
- 1 onion, finely chopped
- 2 cloves garlic, minced
- 2 carrots, diced
- 2 celery stalks, diced
- 1 can (14.5 oz) diced tomatoes
- 6 cups vegetable broth
- 1 tsp cumin
- 1 tsp paprika
- Salt and pepper to taste
- 2 tbsp olive oil
- Fresh parsley, chopped (for garnish)
- Fresh basil leaves (for garnish)

## INSTRUCTIONS

1. Prepare the Ingredients: Rinse the lentils under cold water and set aside. Finely chop the onion, dice the carrots and celery, and mince the garlic.
2. Sauté the Vegetables: In a large pot, heat the olive oil over medium heat. Add the chopped onion, carrots, and celery. Sauté for about 5-7 minutes, or until the vegetables are softened. Add the minced garlic and cook for an additional 1-2 minutes.
3. Cook the Soup: Add the rinsed lentils, diced tomatoes (with their juice), vegetable broth, cumin, paprika, salt, and pepper to the pot. Stir to combine. Bring the mixture to a boil, then reduce the heat to low and simmer for 30-35 minutes, or until the lentils are tender.
4. Serve: Once the lentils are cooked, taste and adjust seasoning if necessary. Ladle the soup into bowls. Garnish with fresh parsley and basil leaves. Serve hot and enjoy your hearty lentil soup.

**Nutritional : Calories: 190 kcal | Protein: 9g | Carbohydrates: 30g | Fat: 4g | Fiber: 12g | Sugar: 5g**

# 88.Rainbow Veggie Bowl with Creamy Tahini Dressing

★★★★★

🕐 **20 Minutes**  ♨🕐 **25 Minutes**  🍴 **4 servings**

## INGREDIENTS

- 1 cup quinoa, rinsed
- 2 cups water
- 1 cup chickpeas, cooked or canned (drained and rinsed)
- 1 cup broccoli florets
- 1 cup diced butternut squash
- 1 red bell pepper, diced
- 1 yellow bell pepper, diced
- 1 cucumber, diced
- 1 cup cherry tomatoes, halved
- 2 tbsp olive oil
- Salt and pepper to taste
- 1 tbsp sesame seeds (optional for garnish)
- Fresh parsley, chopped (for garnish)
- For the Creamy Tahini Dressing:
- 1/4 cup tahini
- 2 tbsp lemon juice
- 1 tbsp olive oil
- 1 clove garlic, minced
- 2-3 tbsp water (to thin the dressing)
- Salt and pepper to taste

## INSTRUCTIONS

1. Cook the Quinoa: In a medium saucepan, combine the quinoa and water. Bring to a boil, then reduce heat to low and cover. Simmer for about 15 minutes, or until the quinoa is tender and water is absorbed. Fluff with a fork and set aside.
2. Roast the Vegetables: Preheat your oven to 200°C (400°F). On a baking sheet, toss the broccoli florets, butternut squash, and bell peppers with olive oil, salt, and pepper. Arrange in a single layer and roast for 20-25 minutes, or until the vegetables are tender and slightly browned.
3. Prepare the Dressing: In a small bowl, whisk together the tahini, lemon juice, olive oil, minced garlic, and water. Season with salt and pepper to taste. Adjust the consistency with more water if needed.
4. Assemble the Bowls: In each serving bowl, arrange a portion of quinoa, roasted vegetables, chickpeas, cucumber, and cherry tomatoes. Drizzle with the creamy tahini dressing.
5. Garnish and Serve: Sprinkle with sesame seeds and fresh parsley. Serve immediately and enjoy your vibrant rainbow veggie bowl!

**Nutritional : Calories: 320 kcal | Protein: 10g | Carbohydrates: 45g | Fat: 12g | Fiber: 8g | Sugar: 7g**

# 89.Spicy Roasted Cauliflower

★★★☆☆

🕐 10 Minutes | 🍳🕐 25 Minutes | 🍴 4 servings

## INGREDIENTS

- 1 large head of cauliflower, cut into florets
- 2 tbsp olive oil
- 1 tsp turmeric powder
- 1 tsp cumin powder
- 1 tsp smoked paprika
- 1/2 tsp chili flakes (adjust to taste)
- Salt and pepper to taste
- Fresh cilantro, chopped (for garnish)
- Lime wedges (for serving)

## INSTRUCTIONS

1. Preheat the Oven: Preheat your oven to 200°C (400°F).
2. Season the Cauliflower: In a large bowl, combine olive oil, turmeric powder, cumin powder, smoked paprika, chili flakes, salt, and pepper. Add the cauliflower florets and toss until well coated with the seasoning mixture.
3. Roast the Cauliflower: Spread the seasoned cauliflower florets in a single layer on a baking sheet. Roast in the preheated oven for 25-30 minutes, or until the cauliflower is tender and golden brown, stirring halfway through.
4. Serve: Transfer the roasted cauliflower to a serving dish. Garnish with fresh chopped cilantro and serve with lime wedges on the side.

**Nutrition : Calories: 120 kcal | Protein: 3g | Carbs: 9g | Fat: 7g | Fiber: 3g | Sugar: 2g**

# 90.Creamy Polenta with Roasted Bell Peppers

★★★☆☆

🕐 15 Minutes | 🍳🕐 30 Minutes | 🍴 4 servings

## INGREDIENTS

- For the Polenta:
- 1 cup polenta (cornmeal)
- 4 cups water or vegetable broth
- 2 tbsp butter or olive oil
- 1/2 cup grated Parmesan cheese (optional)
- Salt and pepper to taste
- For the Roasted Bell Peppers:
- 3 bell peppers (red, yellow, orange), sliced
- 1 medium red onion, sliced
- 2 tbsp olive oil
- 2 cloves garlic, minced
- 1 tsp dried thyme
- Salt and pepper to taste
- Fresh parsley, chopped (for garnish)

## INSTRUCTIONS

1. Preheat the Oven: Preheat your oven to 200°C (400°F).
2. Roast the Bell Peppers: In a large bowl, toss the sliced bell peppers and red onion with olive oil, minced garlic, dried thyme, salt, and pepper. Spread the mixture in a single layer on a baking sheet. Roast in the preheated oven for 25-30 minutes, or until the vegetables are tender and slightly charred, stirring halfway through.
3. Cook the Polenta: In a medium saucepan, bring the water or vegetable broth to a boil. Slowly whisk in the polenta, reducing the heat to low. Continue to stir frequently to prevent lumps. Cook for about 20-25 minutes, or until the polenta is thick and creamy. Stir in the butter or olive oil, grated Parmesan cheese (if using), salt, and pepper.
4. Serve: Spoon the creamy polenta onto serving plates. Top with the roasted bell peppers and onions. Garnish with fresh chopped parsley. Serve immediately.

**Nutrition : Calories: 280 kcal | Protein: 6g | Carbs: 35g | Fat: 14g | Fiber: 4g | Sugar: 5**

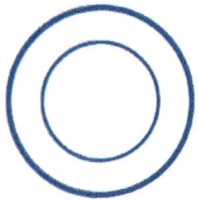 # DESSERT

# 91.Lemon Blueberry Delight

★★★★★

🕐 **15 Minutes**    ♨🕐 **30 Minutes**    🍴 **8 servings**

## INGREDIENTS

- 1 cup almond flour
- 1/4 cup coconut flour
- 1/2 cup erythritol
- 1 tsp baking powder
- 1/4 tsp salt
- 3 large eggs
- 1/2 cup unsweetened almond milk
- 1/4 cup melted coconut oil
- 1 tsp vanilla extract
- 1 tbsp lemon zest
- 1 cup fresh blueberries
- 1/4 cup lemon juice
- 1 cup Greek yogurt
- 1 tbsp chia seeds
- Fresh lemon slices and blueberries for garnish

## INSTRUCTIONS

1. Preheat the Oven: Preheat your oven to 180°C (350°F). Grease and line an 8x8 inch baking pan with parchment paper.
2. Prepare the Dry Ingredients: In a large bowl, whisk together almond flour, coconut flour, erythritol, baking powder, and salt.
3. Mix Wet Ingredients: In another bowl, beat the eggs, almond milk, melted coconut oil, vanilla extract, and lemon zest until well combined.
4. Combine Ingredients: Slowly add the wet ingredients to the dry ingredients, mixing until a smooth batter forms. Gently fold in the blueberries.
5. Bake the Cake: Pour the batter into the prepared baking pan and bake for 25-30 minutes or until a toothpick inserted into the center comes out clean. Allow to cool completely.
6. Prepare the Yogurt Topping: In a bowl, mix Greek yogurt, lemon juice, and chia seeds. Let it sit for 10 minutes to thicken.
7. Assemble the Cake: Spread the yogurt mixture evenly over the cooled cake. Top with fresh lemon slices and blueberries.
8. Serve: Slice and serve chilled. Enjoy your Lemon Blueberry Delight!

**Nutrition : Calories: 150 kcal | Protein: 6 g | Carbs: 12 g | Fat: 9 g | Fiber: 3 g | Sugar: 4 g**

# 92.Rustic Apple Pecan Pie

★★★★★

🕐 **20 Minutes**    ♨🕐 **50 Minutes**    🍴 **8 servings**

## INGREDIENTS

- 1 premade whole wheat pie crust
- 6 cups peeled and sliced apples (Granny Smith or Honeycrisp work well)
- 1/4 cup erythritol
- 1/4 cup brown sugar substitute
- 1 tsp ground cinnamon
- 1/4 tsp ground nutmeg
- 1/4 tsp salt
- 1 tbsp lemon juice
- 1 tsp vanilla extract
- 1/2 cup chopped pecans
- 2 tbsp cornstarch
- 1 tbsp unsalted butter, cut into small pieces
- Whipped cream (optional, for serving)

## INSTRUCTIONS

1. Preheat the Oven: Preheat your oven to 190°C (375°F).
2. Prepare the Filling: In a large bowl, mix together the sliced apples, erythritol, brown sugar substitute, cinnamon, nutmeg, salt, lemon juice, and vanilla extract. Add the cornstarch and mix until the apples are well-coated.
3. Assemble the Pie: Roll out the pie crust and fit it into a 9-inch pie dish. Pour the apple mixture into the crust, spreading it out evenly. Sprinkle the chopped pecans over the top. Dot the filling with the small pieces of butter.
4. Bake the Pie: Cover the edges of the pie crust with foil to prevent burning. Bake in the preheated oven for 45-50 minutes, or until the apples are tender and the filling is bubbly. Remove the foil for the last 15 minutes of baking to allow the crust to brown.
5. Cool and Serve: Let the pie cool for at least 30 minutes before slicing. Serve with a dollop of whipped cream if desired.

**Nutrition : Calories: 230 kcal | Protein: 3 g | Carbs: 36 g | Fat: 10 g | Fiber: 5 g | Sugar: 12 g**

# 93.Strawberry Delight Cake

★★★★★

🕐 15 Minutes     🍳🕐 30 Minutes     🍴 8 servings

## INSTRUCTIONS

1. Preheat the Oven: Preheat your oven to 180°C (350°F). Grease and flour a 9-inch round cake pan.
2. Mix Dry Ingredients: In a large bowl, combine the almond flour, coconut flour, erythritol, baking powder, and salt.
3. Combine Wet Ingredients: In another bowl, whisk together the applesauce, melted coconut oil, eggs, vanilla extract, and almond milk until well blended.
4. Make the Batter: Gradually add the wet ingredients to the dry ingredients, mixing until just combined. Fold in the sliced strawberries.
5. Bake the Cake: Pour the batter into the prepared cake pan. Bake in the preheated oven for 25-30 minutes, or until a toothpick inserted into the center comes out clean.
6. Cool and Serve: Allow the cake to cool in the pan for 10 minutes, then transfer to a wire rack to cool completely. Serve with a dollop of whipped cream if desired.

## INGREDIENTS

- 1 1/2 cups almond flour
- 1/2 cup coconut flour
- 1/4 cup erythritol
- 1 tsp baking powder
- 1/4 tsp salt
- 1/2 cup unsweetened applesauce
- 1/4 cup coconut oil, melted
- 3 large eggs
- 1 tsp vanilla extract
- 1/2 cup unsweetened almond milk
- 1 cup fresh strawberries, sliced
- Whipped cream (optional, for serving)

**Nutrition : Calories: 210 kcal | Protein: 5 g | Carbs: 14 g | Fat: 15 g | Fiber: 4 g | Sugar: 4 g**

# 94.Coconut Mango Ice Cream

★★★★☆

🕐 20 Minutes     🍳🕐 50 Minutes     🍴 8 servings

## INSTRUCTIONS

1. Blend Ingredients: In a blender, combine the coconut milk, erythritol, vanilla extract, and salt. Blend until smooth.
2. Mix in Mango: Stir in the fresh mango chunks.
3. Chill the Mixture: Pour the mixture into an ice cream maker and churn according to the manufacturer's instructions. If you don't have an ice cream maker, pour the mixture into a shallow dish and freeze, stirring every 30 minutes until it reaches your desired consistency.
4. Add Shredded Coconut: Once the ice cream is partially frozen, fold in the shredded coconut.
5. Freeze Until Firm: Transfer the mixture to a lidded container and freeze for at least 4 hours, or until firm.
6. Serve: Scoop the ice cream into bowls and garnish with extra mango chunks and shredded coconut if desired.

## INGREDIENTS

- 2 cups full-fat coconut milk
- 1/4 cup erythritol or preferred sugar substitute
- 1 tsp vanilla extract
- 1 cup fresh mango chunks
- 1/4 cup unsweetened shredded coconut
- Pinch of salt

**Nutrition : Calories: 180 kcal | Protein: 2 g | Carbs: 10 g | Fat: 16 g | Fiber: 2 g | Sugar: 7 g**

# 95.Orange Muffins

★★★★★

🕐 **15 Minutes**     〰🕐 **25 Minutes**    🍴 **12 servings**

## INGREDIENTS

- 1 1/2 cups almond flour
- 1/2 cup coconut flour
- 1/2 cup erythritol or preferred sugar substitute
- 1 tsp baking powder
- 1/2 tsp baking soda
- 1/4 tsp salt
- 3 large eggs
- 1/2 cup unsweetened applesauce
- 1/2 cup freshly squeezed orange juice
- 1/4 cup coconut oil, melted
- 1 tsp vanilla extract
- Zest of 1 orange

## INSTRUCTIONS

1. Preheat the Oven: Preheat your oven to 175°C (350°F). Line a muffin tin with paper liners or lightly grease it.
2. Mix Dry Ingredients: In a large bowl, whisk together the almond flour, coconut flour, erythritol, baking powder, baking soda, and salt.
3. Combine Wet Ingredients: In another bowl, whisk together the eggs, unsweetened applesauce, orange juice, melted coconut oil, vanilla extract, and orange zest until well combined.
4. Combine Wet and Dry Mixtures: Add the wet ingredients to the dry ingredients and stir until just combined. Do not overmix.
5. Fill Muffin Tins: Divide the batter evenly among the prepared muffin cups, filling each about 3/4 full.
6. Bake: Bake in the preheated oven for 20-25 minutes, or until a toothpick inserted into the center of a muffin comes out clean.
7. Cool and Serve: Allow the muffins to cool in the tin for 5 minutes, then transfer to a wire rack to cool completely. Serve warm or at room temperature.

**Nutrition : Calories: 120 kcal | Protein: 5 g | Carbs: 8 g | Fat: 8 g | Fiber: 3 g | Sugar: 3 g**

# 96.Raspberry Crumble Bars

★★★★★

🕐 **20 Minutes**    〰🕐 **50 Minutes**    🍴 **8 servings**

## INGREDIENTS

- 1 cup almond flour
- 1/2 cup coconut flour
- 1/2 cup erythritol or preferred sugar substitute
- 1/2 tsp baking powder
- 1/4 tsp salt
- 1/2 cup unsalted butter, melted
- 1 large egg
- 1 tsp vanilla extract
- 2 cups fresh raspberries
- 1 tbsp lemon juice
- 1 tbsp cornstarch

## INSTRUCTIONS

1. Preheat the Oven: Preheat your oven to 175°C (350°F). Line an 8x8 inch baking pan with parchment paper, leaving an overhang for easy removal.
2. Prepare the Crust and Crumble: In a large bowl, whisk together the almond flour, coconut flour, erythritol, baking powder, and salt. Add the melted butter, egg, and vanilla extract, and stir until the mixture forms a crumbly dough.
3. Form the Base: Press 2/3 of the dough mixture firmly into the prepared baking pan to form an even layer.
4. Prepare the Raspberry Filling: In a medium bowl, toss the raspberries with lemon juice and cornstarch until well coated. Spread the raspberry mixture evenly over the crust in the baking pan.
5. Add the Crumble Topping: Sprinkle the remaining dough mixture over the raspberries to form a crumble topping.
6. Bake: Bake in the preheated oven for 30-35 minutes, or until the top is golden brown and the raspberry filling is bubbly.
7. Cool and Serve: Allow the bars to cool completely in the pan before lifting them out using the parchment overhang. Cut into 12 bars and serve.

**Nutrition: Calories: 160 kcal | Protein: 3 g | Carbs: 8 g | Fat: 14 g | Fiber: 4 g | Sugar: 3 g**

# 97.Key Lime Pie with Whipped Cream

★★★★★

🕐 **20 Minutes**　　♨🕐 **15 Minutes**　　🍴 **8 servings**

## INGREDIENTS

- Crust:
- 1 1/2 cups almond flour
- 1/4 cup melted butter
- 2 tbsp erythritol or preferred sugar substitute
- Filling:
- 1/2 cup fresh lime juice
- 1 tbsp lime zest
- 4 large egg yolks
- 1 can (14 oz) sweetened condensed milk (use a sugar-free version for diabetics)
- Topping:
- 1 cup heavy whipping cream
- 2 tbsp powdered erythritol or preferred sugar substitute
- Lime slices for garnish

## INSTRUCTIONS

1. Preheat the Oven: Preheat your oven to 175°C (350°F).
2. Prepare the Crust: In a medium bowl, mix almond flour, melted butter, and erythritol until combined. Press the mixture firmly into the bottom and up the sides of a 9-inch pie dish. Bake for 10 minutes, then let it cool completely.
3. Prepare the Filling: In a large bowl, whisk together the lime juice, lime zest, egg yolks, and sweetened condensed milk until smooth and well combined.
4. Bake the Pie: Pour the filling into the cooled crust. Bake in the preheated oven for 15 minutes or until the filling is set. Allow the pie to cool to room temperature, then refrigerate for at least 2 hours or until chilled.
5. Prepare the Whipped Cream: In a large bowl, beat the heavy whipping cream and powdered erythritol with an electric mixer on high speed until stiff peaks form.
6. Serve: Garnish the pie with whipped cream and lime slices before serving.

**Nutrition : Calories: 250 kcal | Protein: 6 g | Carbs: 12 g | Fat: 20 g | Fiber: 2 g | Sugar: 5 g**

# 98.Mango Panna Cotta

★★★★☆

🕐 **20 Minutes**　　♨🕐 **10 Minutes**　　🍴 **4 servings**

## INGREDIENTS

- 1 cup heavy cream
- 1 cup coconut milk
- 2 tbsp powdered erythritol or preferred sweetener
- 1 tsp vanilla extract
- 1 packet unflavored gelatin (about 2 1/4 tsp)
- 2 tbsp water
- 1 cup mango puree
- 1/2 cup fresh mango cubes
- Fresh mint leaves for garnish

## INSTRUCTIONS

1. Prepare the Gelatin: In a small bowl, sprinkle the gelatin over the water and let it sit for about 5 minutes to bloom.
2. Heat the Cream Mixture: In a medium saucepan, combine the heavy cream, coconut milk, and erythritol. Heat over medium heat until it starts to simmer, stirring occasionally.
3. Add the Gelatin: Remove the saucepan from heat and stir in the bloomed gelatin until it is completely dissolved. Add the vanilla extract and mix well.
4. Pour into Molds: Divide the mixture evenly among four serving glasses or molds. Let it cool to room temperature, then refrigerate for at least 4 hours, or until set.
5. Add Mango Puree: Once the panna cotta has set, pour a layer of mango puree over each serving. Top with fresh mango cubes.
6. Garnish and Serve: Garnish each serving with fresh mint leaves before serving. Enjoy your refreshing Mango Panna Cotta!

**Nutrition : Calories: 200 kcal | Protein: 3 g | Carbs: 10 g | Fat: 18 g | Fiber: 1 g | Sugar: 8 g**

# 99.Raspberry Crumble Bars

★★★★★

🕐 15 Minutes   ♨🕐 12 Minutes   🍴 24 servings

## INGREDIENTS

- 1 cup almond flour
- 1/4 cup coconut flour
- 1/2 cup butter, softened
- 1/2 cup erythritol or preferred sugar substitute
- 1 large egg
- 1 tsp vanilla extract
- 1/2 tsp baking powder
- 1/4 tsp salt
- 1/2 cup chopped almonds
- 1/4 cup sugar-free white chocolate chips (optional)

## INSTRUCTIONS

1. Preheat the Oven: Preheat your oven to 175°C (350°F). Line a baking sheet with parchment paper.
2. Mix the Dry Ingredients: In a medium bowl, combine almond flour, coconut flour, baking powder, and salt. Set aside.
3. Cream the Butter and Sweetener: In a large bowl, beat the softened butter and erythritol until light and fluffy. Add the egg and vanilla extract, and mix until well combined.
4. Combine Ingredients: Gradually add the dry ingredients to the wet ingredients, mixing until a dough forms. Fold in the chopped almonds and white chocolate chips if using.
5. Form the Cookies: Scoop tablespoon-sized balls of dough and place them on the prepared baking sheet. Flatten each ball slightly with your palm.
6. Bake the Cookies: Bake in the preheated oven for 10-12 minutes, or until the edges are golden brown. Allow the cookies to cool on the baking sheet for a few minutes before transferring them to a wire rack to cool completely.
7. Serve: Enjoy your delicious almond cookies with a cup of tea or coffee.

**Nutrition : Calories: 250 kcal | Protein: 6 g | Carbs: 12 g | Fat: 20 g | Fiber: 2 g | Sugar: 5 g**

# 100.Berry Chia Pudding

★★★★★

🕐 10 Minutes   ♨🕐 240 Minutes   🍴 4 servings

## INGREDIENTS

- 1/2 cup chia seeds
- 2 cups unsweetened almond milk
- 1 tsp vanilla extract
- 1 tbsp maple syrup (optional, adjust for sweetness)
- 1 cup mixed berries (raspberries, blueberries, blackberries)
- Fresh mint leaves for garnish

## INSTRUCTIONS

1. In a mixing bowl, combine chia seeds, almond milk, vanilla extract, and maple syrup.
2. Stir well to ensure the chia seeds are evenly distributed and not clumping together.
3. Cover the bowl and refrigerate for at least 4 hours or overnight to allow the chia seeds to absorb the liquid and form a pudding-like consistency.
4. Once set, divide the chia pudding into serving glasses.
5. Top with fresh mixed berries and garnish with mint leaves.
6. Serve chilled and enjoy!

**Nutrition : Calories: 120 kcal | Protein: 4 g | Carbs: 16 g | Fat: 6 g | Fiber: 10 g | Sugar: 6 g**

# 28 -Day Meal Plan

| Day | Breakfast | Lunch | Dinner | Snacks |
|---|---|---|---|---|
| 1 | 1. Toast with Guacamole and Fried Egg Yolk | 16. Quinoa and Black Bean Salad with Avocado and Lime | 62. Grilled Lemon Herb Chicken Breast | 11. Blueberry Mint Smoothie |
| 2 | 2. Spinach and Feta Egg Muffins | 17. White Bean and Kale Stew | 37. Grilled Salmon Fillet with Lemon and Dill | 10. Hummus with Fresh Veggie Sticks |
| 3 | 3. Greek Yogurt Oat Pancakes | 18. Brown Rice and Vegetable Stir-Fry with Tofu | 65. Beef and Broccoli Stir-Fry | 15. Greek Yogurt and Spiced Apples |
| 4 | 4. Overnight Oats with Blueberries and Almonds | 19. Quinoa Tabbouleh Salad | 43. Herb-Crusted Cod with Asparagus | 7. Avocado and Egg Breakfast Salad |
| 5 | 5. Veggie-Packed Omelette | 20. Three-Bean Vegetable Stew | 73. Grilled Pork Chop with Peach Glaze | 99. Almond Cookies |
| 6 | 6. Whole Wheat Waffles with Fresh Berries | 21. Fresh Tomato and Onion Salad | 42. Grilled Shrimp Skewers with Vegetables | 97. Raspberry Crumble Bars |
| 7 | 7. Avocado and Egg Breakfast Salad | 22. Spiced Pumpkin Soup | 74. Grilled Chicken Salad | 98. Key Lime Pie with Whipped Cream |
| 8 | 8. Mushroom and Herb Frittata | 23. Spring Vegetable Ribollita | 82. Grilled Steak with Roasted Vegetables | 100. Mango Panna Cotta |
| 9 | 9. Avocado Toast with Cherry Tomatoes | 24. Black Bean and Veggie Burrito | 83. Roasted Chicken Breast with Pumpkin and Spinach | 86. Buckwheat Salad with Cherry Tomatoes and Red Onion |
| 10 | 10. Hummus with Fresh Veggie Sticks | 25. Mediterranean Chickpea Salad with Feta and Olives | 38. Grilled Lemon Garlic Salmon | 96. Orange Muffins |

| | | | |
|---|---|---|---|
| **11** | 11. Blueberry Mint Smoothie | 26. Lentil Soup with Carrots, Celery, and Spinach | 67. Herb Fried Chicken | 95. Coconut Mango Ice Cream |
| **12** | 12. Broccoli and Cheese Frittata | 27. Grilled Zucchini Ribbons with Fresh Herbs | 79. Beef Bourguignon with Carrots and Onions | 29. Fresh Tomato, Cucumber, and Lettuce Salad with Flax Seeds |
| **13** | 13. Stacked Pancakes with Berries | 28. Avocado, Tomato, and Feta Salad | 76. Honey Mustard Glazed Chicken Thighs | 94. Strawberry Delight Cake |
| **14** | 14. Oatmeal Served with Yogurt and Fresh Fruit | 34. Zucchini Noodles with Tomatoes and Basil | 46. Grilled Tilapia with Citrus Vinaigrette | 93. Rustic Apple Pecan Pie |
| **15** | 15. Greek Yogurt and Spiced Apples | 35. Vegan Stuffed Bell Peppers with Quinoa and Black Beans | 47. Grilled Swordfish with Lemon Herb Butter | 90. Spicy Roasted Cauliflower |
| **16** | 1. Toast with Guacamole and Fried Egg Yolk | 48. Grilled Tilapia with Asparagus and Pesto | 52. Grilled Shrimp Tacos with Avocado Salsa | 92. Lemon Blueberry Delight |
| **17** | 2. Spinach and Feta Egg Muffins | 37. Grilled Salmon Fillet with Lemon and Dill | 49. Pan-Seared Salmon with Garlic Sautéed Kale | 99. Almond Cookies |
| **18** | 3. Greek Yogurt Oat Pancakes | 26. Lentil Soup with Carrots, Celery, and Spinach | 70. Stuffed Bell Peppers | 97. Raspberry Crumble Bars |
| **19** | 4. Overnight Oats with Blueberries and Almonds | 25. Mediterranean Chickpea Salad with Feta and Olives | 85. Roasted Beef with Mashed Potatoes | 98. Key Lime Pie with Whipped Cream |
| **20** | 5. Veggie-Packed Omelette | 28. Avocado, Tomato, and Feta Salad | 75. Grilled Sausages with Mashed Potatoes and Onion Gravy | 86. Buckwheat Salad with Cherry Tomatoes and Red Onion |
| **21** | 6. Whole Wheat Waffles with Fresh Berries | 34. Zucchini Noodles with Tomatoes and Basil | 62. Grilled Lemon Herb Chicken Breast | 96. Orange Muffins |

| | | | | |
|---|---|---|---|---|
| **22** | 7. Avocado and Egg Breakfast Salad | 27. Grilled Zucchini Ribbons with Fresh Herbs | 71. Malai Chicken with Yogurt Sauce | 95. Coconut Mango Ice Cream |
| **23** | 8. Mushroom and Herb Frittata | 22. Spiced Pumpkin Soup | 48. Grilled Tilapia with Asparagus and Pesto | 29. Fresh Tomato, Cucumber, and Lettuce Salad with Flax Seeds |
| **24** | 9. Avocado Toast with Cherry Tomatoes | 20. Three-Bean Vegetable Stew | 43. Herb-Crusted Cod with Asparagus | 92. Lemon Blueberry Delight |
| **25** | 10. Hummus with Fresh Veggie Sticks | 23. Spring Vegetable Ribollita | 76. Honey Mustard Glazed Chicken Thighs | 93. Rustic Apple Pecan Pie |
| **26** | 11. Blueberry Mint Smoothie | 24. Black Bean and Veggie Burrito | 82. Grilled Steak with Roasted Vegetables | 94. Strawberry Delight Cake |
| **27** | 12. Broccoli and Cheese Frittata | 21. Fresh Tomato and Onion Salad | 47. Grilled Swordfish with Lemon Herb Butter | 90. Spicy Roasted Cauliflower |
| **28** | 13. Stacked Pancakes with Berries | 19. Quinoa Tabbouleh Salad | 52. Grilled Shrimp Tacos with Avocado Salsa | 91. Creamy Polenta with Roasted Bell Peppers |

# I kindly and wholeheartedly ask that if you enjoyed the work, please leave a review.

## Your Exclusive Bonus:

### - Video Recipes with Step-by-Step Explanations

SCAN ME

Printed in Great Britain
by Amazon